MY JERUSALEM STREET CATS

Their Personalities and Social Behavior

RAPHAELLA BILSKI

PREPRESS EDITION

My Jerusalem Street Cats

Their Personalities and Social Behavior

Raphaella Bilski

*Illustrations by
David Cohen*

*Translated from Hebrew by
Shlomit Harrosh*

 SAMUEL WACHTMAN'S SONS  DEKEL PUBLISHING HOUSE

My Jerusalem Street Cats
Their Personalities and Social Behavior

Raphaella Bilski
Copyright © 2014

Dekel Publishing House
www.dekelpublishing.com

North American rights by
Samuel Wachtman's Sons, Inc.
ISBN 978-1-888820-72-0

All rights reserved. No portion of this book, except for brief review, may be reproduced, stored in a retrieval system, or transmitted in any form or by any means – electronic, mechanical, photocopying, recording, or otherwise – without written permission of the publisher. For information regarding international rights please contact Dekel Publishing House, Israel; for North American rights please contact Samuel Wachtman's Sons, Inc., U.S.A.

English translation:	Shlomit Harrosh
Language editing:	Kathleen Roman
Illustrations:	David Cohen

Cover image: Kittens © Countrymama, Dreamstime.com

Cover design and typesetting by

For information contact:

Dekel Publishing House
P.O. Box 45094
Tel Aviv 6145002, Israel
Tel: +972 3506-3235
Fax: +972 3506-7332
Email: info@dekelpublishing.com

Samuel Wachtman's Sons, Inc.
2460 Garden Road, Suite C
Monterey, CA 93940, U.S.A.
Tel: 831 649-0669
Fax: 831 649-8007
Email: samuelwachtman@gmail.com

In memory of my mother Vera Bilski,

who made me an animal-loving person,

and to Shon the cat for being what he is.

Table of Contents

Introduction 9

Family Trees 12
    Kitsushi's Family 12
    Beauty's Family 13
    Tricolor's Family and Cats Who Arrived Alone 14

Chapter 1   What Do I Have to Do with Cats? 15

Chapter 2   The First Family 20

Chapter 3   Courageous Cats 37
    Fluffy: The Courageous Fur Ball 38
    Sasha: The Brave Cat 45
    Sophie: The Cat with Seven Souls 48

Chapter 4   A Tale of Pishoosh, Shushka, and Friendship
                Between Cats 56

Chapter 5   Motherhood and Joint Motherhood 71

Chapter 6   Beauty and Colomina: A Mother-Daughter Friendship 89

Chapter 7   The One and Only Nonny 105

Chapter 8	Furry and Bambi, and a Little about Some Other Furries and Bambies	122
Chapter 9	The Silver Cat	135
Chapter 10	Grayush: The Pavarotti of Cats	139
Chapter 11	A Short but Happy Life	150
	Tete the Duchess	150
	A Cat Named Legs	155
	Toto: The Cat that Fell from the Sky	160
Chapter 12	The Pergola Cats: Turquoise and Pizzo	165
Chapter 13	The Pergola Infiltrators: Cloud and Red	180
Chapter 14	Cats by Coat Color	187
	Tricolor Females and Ginger Males	187
	Black and White Cats	206
Chapter 15	Unusual Cats with Ordinary Names	213
	Green Cat	213
	White Cat	217
Chapter 16	Being a Leader	221
Chapter 17	Dying Cats	234
Chapter 18	So Now What?	239
Acknowledgments		242

Introduction

This book spans a period of fourteen years, beginning in 1993. At that time, there was almost no awareness of the situation of street cats in Israel. For example, there was only one serious animal welfare society concerned with animal rights and providing advice to caregivers. Contacting this society wasn't easy. Unlike today, when a message posted on Facebook can reach hundreds if not thousands of people within minutes, in Israel in the 1990s there was no way to contact other animal lovers via the internet. So during most of the period described in this book, I worked alone, relying only on the help of a neighbor and my local veterinarian.

The most serious consequence of the absence of animal welfare societies in Israel at the time was the lack of cat catchers to neuter and spay street cats. Only in extreme situations, when a dog or a cat bit someone, would an animal catcher arrive, brandishing a pole tipped with a wire noose. The trapping process was horrifying to see. Needless to say, I was unable to catch the cats by myself and bring them to the vet to be neutered or spayed. I only rarely succeeded in doing so, and only with particularly friendly cats. This explains the number of births in my community of street cats and its rapid growth rate.

The situation of street cats in Israel changed with the Israeli supreme court's decision of 2004 concerning street cats, known as the "Cats Ruling" (Judgment 48884/00). The supreme court ruled that street cats have the right to live in the streets and that people are allowed to feed them provided that the following four conditions are met:

1. The feeding area is kept clean.
2. Cats are fed only dry cat food.
3. Cats are fed in a secluded area not easily seen by passers-by.
4. Cats are caught using humanitarian methods to be spayed or neutered, vaccinated for rabies, and then returned to their original habitat.

The Supreme Court decreed that it is prohibited to kill a street cat or move the cat from its original habitat unless the cat constitutes a serious health risk and it is only done as a last resort after all other options failed. Should this be the case, the cat may legally be destroyed, but it must be captured and killed by a professional animal catcher to ensure the cat does not suffer.

The Israeli Supreme Court's decision of 2004 concerning street cats became official policy, spelled out in the Ministry of Agriculture and Rural Development's policy paper "Procedure for the Treatment of the Street Cat." The situation of street cats in Israel is still far from ideal, as municipal authorities lack the necessary budget to spay or neuter all street cats within their jurisdiction. Only about a third of street cats in Israel are fixed. In addition, there is no official census regarding street cats in Israel. An unofficial estimate given to me in personal communications with the head of Jerusalem's veterinarians lists about forty thousand street cats in Jerusalem and about three-hundred thousand street cats in Israel.

Introduction

The conditions that prevailed during the years described in this book made it possible for an impressive cat community to develop in my garden in Jerusalem. I believe that this community provides a unique perspective on the social lives of cats. Written chronologically, this book relates the growth of my understanding of the way relationships develop between the cats and how a community evolves. The book also recounts the cats' relationships with me. Individual chapters describe the character and conduct of the most remarkable cats, focusing on behaviors and experiences that can only occur in a community, such as leadership, joint motherhood, friendship, mentorship, and organization.

Most cat lovers don't notice these behavior patterns because they cannot be discerned if one merely feeds stray cats on the street or has pet cats at home. And therein lays the value of this book. It is my hope that this book will increase readers' awareness not only of the plight of these animals, but also of the wonder that is the life of the street cat.

Family Trees

Kitsushi's Family

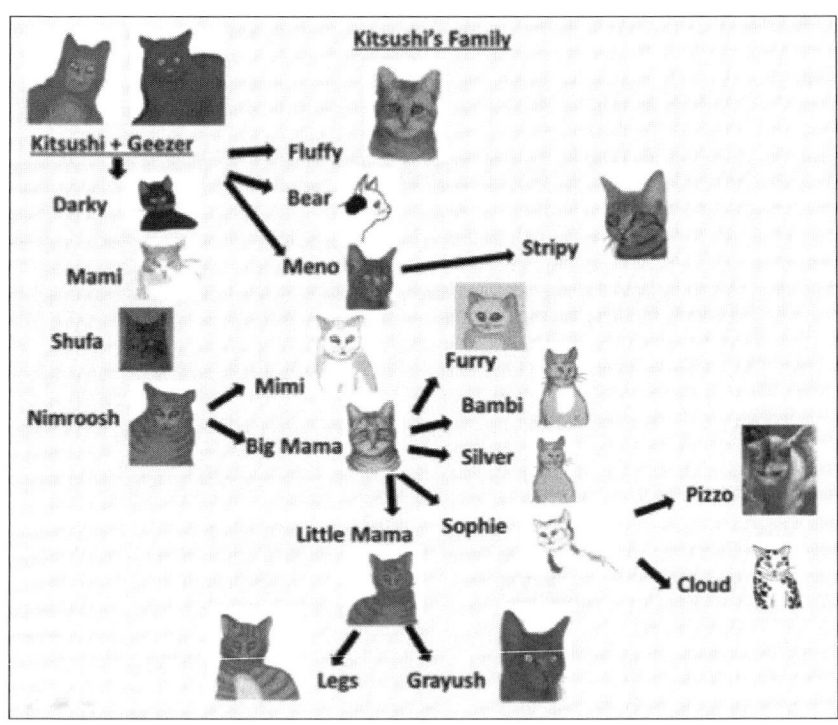

Beauty's Family

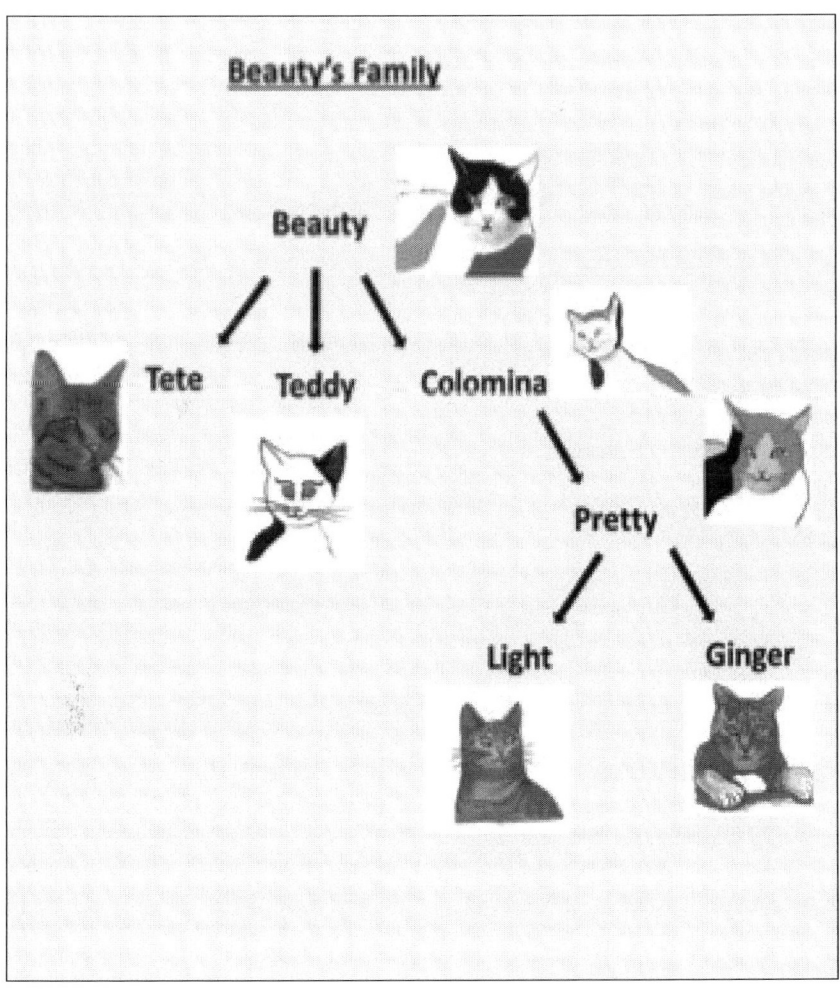

Tricolor's Family and Cats Who Arrived Alone

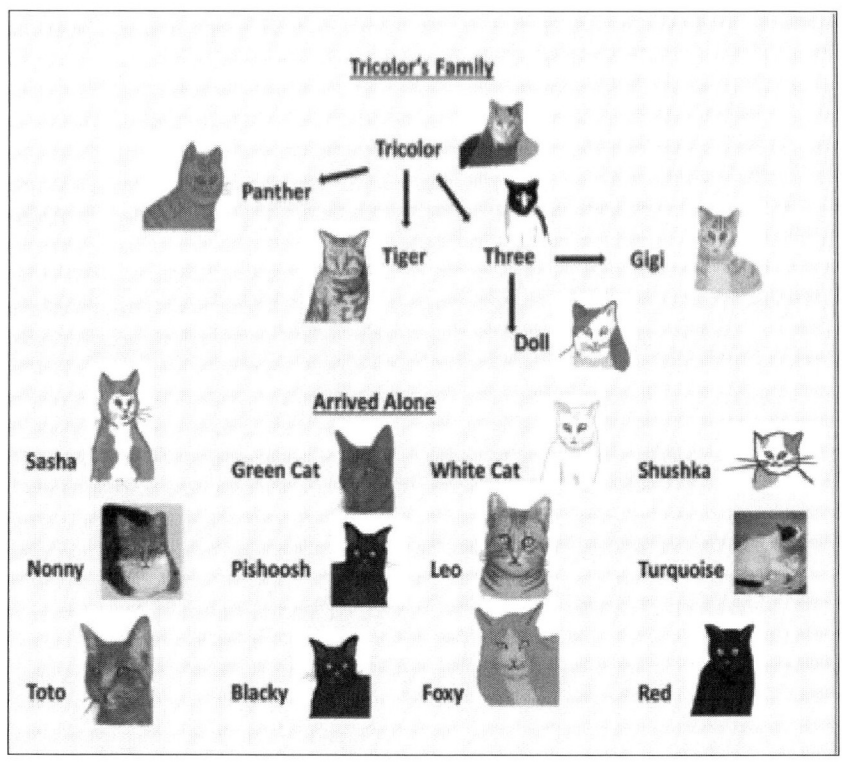

Chapter 1:
What Do I Have to Do with Cats?

I have often heard that many believe people fall into one of two categories: dog people versus cat people.

I grew up with a dog in our home from a very young age. My first dog, Mooki, arrived when I was four years old and lived with us for only six years. Mooki had the misfortune of being pushed into a fountain in Dizengoff Square (the center of Tel Aviv once upon a time). As a result, he contracted a kidney infection and never recovered.

A long time passed before Sandy, our second dog, arrived. I think the trauma of Mooki's premature death was not something my mother, Mooki's primary caregiver, wanted to relive.

However, when I was nineteen years old and serving in the army, my uncle's miniature pinscher gave birth. I fell in love with one of the puppies and begged my parents to let me keep her. My mother, always the animal lover, agreed, and, like all adolescents, I promised to take full responsibility for Alexandra, who I had already nicknamed Sandy. I promised to wake up early each morning and walk her, and to care for her when she got sick. I don't think that my mother took my promises seriously, but seeing that I truly wanted the dog, she agreed.

Of course it ended up being my mother who took Sandy for a walk each morning. In fact, the responsibility for Sandy's care fell mostly on her. But when Sandy contracted a serious disease when she was six, I ran with her to the veterinarian countless times and cared for her faithfully until she recovered.

When I left for England for my doctoral studies, my first question in every letter and phone call was always, "How is Sandy?"

When Sandy died at the age of sixteen and some months, I was heartbroken. Since I was living in Jerusalem at the time, having settled there upon my return from England, I postponed visiting my parents' home in Tel-Aviv, afraid that I wouldn't be able to bear being home without Sandy.

I adopted my third dog, Blacky, a black and white mutt, when I was thirty-seven and quickly realized that either my home didn't suit him or he simply didn't like the place. Blacky destroyed everything that could be destroyed and bit me countless times on my arms and legs. When I took him for a walk, he would occasionally manage to escape, leash in tow, and disappear for hours. I understood that Blacky needed space. With help from the then-head of the Israeli Society for Prevention of Cruelty to Animals, new owners were found for Blacky in an agricultural village. In his new home Blacky had all the space he needed. I am not proud of my failure with Blacky, but sometimes a pair just has to admit that they aren't a good match and find a better alternative.

My husband and I adopted my fourth dog, a magnificent rottweiler named Kato, when I was forty-one. During the first six months of his life, Kato was raised by a dog trainer, who also took care of the unsavory business of housebreaking him. So it was that Kato came to our house full trained.

I loved him as I had loved Sandy. This time I was the primary caretaker and when Kato fell ill at the age of nine and we had to put him to sleep, I mourned his loss for a long time. On the face of it, then, one might think that I am a dog person. But that would be a mistake.

Ever since I can remember, my mother raised me to love both dogs and cats. We lived in a spacious second-floor condo on stilts in Tel-Aviv. Every day my mother would go down to feed the street cats and give medicine to any who were sick. I would usually accompany her, and everyone on our street knew Vera Bilski and her daughter Raphaella's obsession with street cats.

With my mother, I took part in challenging operations like saving kittens that had fallen and become trapped, fishing them out of water-filled holes in the winter, drying them, and feeding them. My mother never stopped taking care of street cats—not even when Mooki or Sandy lived with us.

My mother's great love of dogs and cats was a beautiful expression of her all-encompassing love for animals in general. The compassion she had for street cats must have been passed down to me through genes and education.

Undoubtedly there is a marked difference between raising a dog or a cat at home and caring for numerous street cats. Pets in one's home become part of the family; their lives become interwoven with the life of the household. Caring for street cats is nothing like this. In this book, I want to share my experience of caring for dozens of street cats. I hope readers are not only those who already care for street cats to some extent, but also people who know nothing about them.

After years of caring for street cats, I have come to see them as a society parallel to our own. They live around us; they depend on us; but we can also learn to enjoy their company.

At first, I thought of writing a more sociological-ethological book about street cats. However, I came to realize that my true ambition is to reach as wide a readership as possible, and simply to introduce readers to the world of street cats. I believe that when one becomes better acquainted with the life of street cats through books like this, something in one's heart softens. There is no doubt that awareness of street cats has been growing over the past few years, mainly due to the work of nonprofit organizations. But it is not enough.

Whenever I walk down a street or a particular neighborhood in Jerusalem, I can immediately tell whether the place has feeding stations for cats or people who care for them. If there are neglected and scrawny-looking cats huddled near trash cans, it's obvious to me that, unfortunately, their territory lacks caregivers. When trash cans are deserted and cats can be seen in yards, or on rare occasions on the sidewalk, walking with their tails erect, I know that they are being cared for.

But this should not mislead readers. This book was not written just to improve society's attitude toward street cats. It was first and foremost written with all my heart and mind as a book of love and appreciation—my love and appreciation for the many street cats that I have cared for, and their love and appreciation for me. More than anything, I want to tell readers of the amazing qualities and fascinating lives of the cats whose stories fill the pages of this book.

This is a book about a great love. Like all great loves it is full of joy mixed with sadness, satisfaction mixed with pain, and immense and time-consuming devotion.

Not long ago, I put Colomina to sleep. She was a beautiful female cat and a member of the community of street cats that I care for. For over ten years she walked around the neighborhood with her beautiful tail held high, the picture of health and dignity.

Colomina had a wonderful life full of kittens. Most of them survived, and they and their offspring and relatives form a large part of the community of cats that I feed to this day. With Colomina's death, I come full circle, since she was the last surviving member of the first generation of cats that arrived in my garden fourteen years ago. As we shall see, Colomina was not a member of the first family that appeared at my place, but her mother, Beauty, who died six months ago, started the second family in my community of cats, and as far as I'm concerned Colomina was a member of the founding generation.

Colomina

It was the death of Colomina, the last of the founding generation, that drove me to sit and write about these cats—to write of their lives, characters, behavior, and relationships—with each other and with me—which I've learned over time do, in fact, exist.

Chapter 2: The First Family

The events described in this book take place in a neighborhood in Jerusalem called Beit HaKerem. Jerusalem is one of the most beautiful cities in the world. One of its weaknesses is that Jerusalem is separated into different neighborhoods, each one almost self-sufficient. The center of the city that is accessible to all is, in my opinion, much too small.

However, Beit HaKerem is a western neighborhood, one of the oldest but modern in design. Its beauty is especially remarkable because of the huge trees that grow there. These trees are protected nature in the area.

My house—a three-story, medium-sized building—is surrounded by a relatively huge garden and yard. Our street is small and quiet, the ideal location for cats. Indeed a lot of cats have come to live on our street. In Israel, street cats make up the majority of the country's cat population. The weather is a contributing factor as well.

In March of 1993, my dog Kato passed away. During the nine years he lived, no cat dared set foot in our enclosed garden. After Kato's death, I couldn't bear to take in another dog. My love for him had been so fierce and his death had been such a blow that I decided I would never adopt another animal.

Beit HaKerem

One morning, a few months after Kato had passed, I went out to the garden, as I always do during the spring and summer. At that time, the garden was spacious and surrounded by a fence, one small section shaded by the second-floor balcony and paved, and the larger section covered with grass and plants. I refer to this location throughout this book simply as "the garden." Four and a half years later we built a closed pergola for humans in the garden with an open cat pergola right next to it. The remaining area, which is quite sizeable, is covered with gravel and plants, including a small fishpond, all of which is enclosed by a green hedge. I refer to this section simply as "the yard."

I had just sat down on a rattan armchair when suddenly a female cat appeared, the spitting image of an Egyptian cat, though her coat was bluish gray.

Beit HaKerem

With perfect aplomb, she emitted a single meow and then waited. It seemed that she knew I would feed her. And so I did. I returned indoors and took some leftovers from the refrigerator, since at that time of course I didn't have any cat food in the house.

After she finished eating the cat jumped out of the garden, and I thought I would never see her again. Clearly, at this early stage, I was completely ignorant of the ways of cats, especially when it came to the smart ones.

But I was intrigued. The next day I went out to check if the cat had reappeared in the garden. And what did I see if not the Egyptian gray cat accompanied by what appeared to be kittens.

At this point I didn't even know what the kittens looked like or how many there were since the mother carefully kept them away from me, gesturing and hissing threateningly when I tried to come closer.

Kitsushi

Since I had been raised to love animals, as I've already mentioned, I quickly went to the supermarket to buy cat food. I bought a few boxes of canned food and a bag of dry food. I also got some disposable plates and water bowls. As an afterthought, I added a few packages of cottage cheese. I returned home with all this goodness and prepared a magnificent feast on one plate for the cat that I'd already named, quite unoriginally, Kitsushi. (Children of Russian extraction sometimes call a cat *kitsushi*, which means "kitten.")

I put the plate down in the garden, but it was only after I had shut the door between the house to the garden that I saw Kitsushi approach the food and eat it leisurely. Afterward she produced a sound that I came to later recognize as one that mother cats use to call their kittens. At her call, four kittens, which I had so far seen only from afar, ran to their mother and the plate. They were too small to eat the dry food that I had brought, but from where I was standing, it seemed they were eating, or more precisely, nibbling, a bit of the wet food. Since this was happening at quite some distance, I could only guess that the meal was over when all five cats suddenly disappeared, taking shelter under one of the bushes, perhaps, or inside the many flowerpots and containers strewn around the garden.

Thus with one small family my love affair with these street cats began. I never imagined that I would end up turning the garden into a feeding and caring station for street cats. Kitsushi was a most interesting mother; two weeks passed before she let me watch her nurse her kittens. Naturally she still maintained a reasonable distance between us and waited for me to disappear behind the glass door, from where I was able to watch without posing a threat.

However, her budding trust in me was expressed when she permitted me to see her lie down in various strange positions with the four kittens attached to her. She stayed behind a great bush most of the time but let me see her occasionally by moving in front of the bush.

As time passed, I learned to tell the kittens apart despite the distance and the door that separated us. I named the black kitten Darky. I named another kitten, this one grayish white, Mami (a common endearment in Hebrew similar to "sweetie"), as he seemed to have a very pleasant nature. The other two, which turned out to be females, were typical gray tabbies, the most common type of street cat. I named the larger of the two Nimroosh (small leopard) and the smallest one Shufa.

The First Family

Day by day, Kitsushi's trust in me grew, and she allowed me to come close to her kittens. By then they had grown a bit and had started playing the wonderful games of cats together. They had no need for toys from a pet store. What could be more interesting than wrestling with a sibling, chasing and trying to catch a bug, or displaying an entire repertoire of strange leaps and jumps while playing with a flower?

From Kitsushi I learned that smart cats know how to use their front paws as hands. They insert a paw into a can, for example, scoop out the food, and bring it to their mouths.

Over time the kittens began to eat by themselves and to nurse less frequently. I bought even larger plates, and three times a day I presented myself before "her highness" with a plate heaped high. Sometimes she would eat alone at first and chase her kittens away, allowing them to approach the plate only when she had finished. Other times all of them would begin eating together.

I had already named all the cats, but I still wasn't sure which were male and which were female. As it turned out, I had guessed right. The males, Darky and Mami, were not afraid of me and approached me freely, allowing me to pet them. They even appeared to be somewhat attached to me. The females, Nimroosh and Shufa, however, kept their distance.

Petting and playing with the cats—especially with Mami, who was extraordinarily friendly—was a highly pleasurable experience, both emotionally and tactilely.

And so two months passed, until one bright day I went out into the garden with the cats' usual sumptuous breakfast, only to find the area completely empty of felines. The entire family had disappeared as if swallowed by the earth. I searched every hiding place in the garden. I went outside and searched the street, but to no avail. With a heavy heart I returned home and it's possible that I may have cried a little. I had grown attached to this wonderful family.

Two days passed, during which I went out into the garden at least three times a day to see if by some miracle the family had returned. But neither a miracle nor a single cat was to be found in the garden. I kept thinking of what might have happened to them, and being a pessimist by nature I imagined the very worst: the kittens must have been devoured by a mongoose (we have these creatures around here), or Kitsushi must have taken the kittens to a new location and abandoned them because they were growing up so fast, and the kittens must have been unable to find their way back to the garden—and so on.

On the fourth day I came outside, and lo and behold, the entire family was there waiting for me! Kitsushi seemed content and utterly calm, while the kittens looked like they had returned from a grueling but interesting journey. They devoured the food as if they hadn't eaten at all, or very little, during the past few days. I expected them to disappear again, but life returned to normal.

I asked Kitsushi where they had been—even after only a few months I had gotten into the habit of talking to the cats—when it suddenly dawned on me that she had taken them on what to this day I call "border patrol." It means that Kitsushi took the kittens on a long walk to acquaint them with all the gardens and roads within her territory.

In time, I learned that experienced mothers take their kittens on such a journey because they want the kittens to find their own place within the territory when they grow up. It is also a way of ensuring that the kittens do not attempt to enter areas outside their territory, where they risk serious attacks by other cat families that regard their area as their very own little piece of heaven.

Kittens that come to know their territory well have a significantly higher chance of surviving after being forced to leave their birthplace. Unfortunately, however, some new mothers keep their kittens where they were born and never acquaint them with their surroundings. This difficult task then falls to the kittens themselves when they reach the age of five months or so. As a result, many of them are run over since they never learned what a road is, although, if truth be told, roads are a problem even for experienced cats.

But let's return to our family. Little by little, I began noticing that Kitsushi was leaving the kittens for increasingly longer periods, and that the kittens were getting used to being on their own. They would approach me and the plate by themselves, and they didn't appear to be at all traumatized. In this way, Kitsushi raised the kittens to be independent.

Mami

When the kittens reached two months of age, I asked a veterinarian I knew to make a house call so he could vaccinate the kittens. Since at least two kittens, Mami and Darky, let me come close to them and touch them, I thought this event wouldn't be too complicated, at least for these two. Mami was even in the habit of sitting on my lap in the garden and letting me hold him in my arms! But it turned out to be an impossible task. The moment the kittens spotted the vet, they scattered in every direction and all attempts to entice them back and convince them to let me hold them while the veterinarian administered the shots failed miserably. Kitsushi was absent the whole time, having left on one of her excursions.

Autumn had begun. I went to the pet store and bought two "houses" for the cats. I think I was one of very few people who turned covered litter boxes into cat houses. I came up with the idea on my own, as it gave the cats more security and warmth. I padded the houses with my old sweaters and placed them under the roof against the wall. The kittens learned to sleep in the houses, though they always preferred to huddle together in one house. Their preferred house was located near the entrance to the living room, so they weren't troubled by rain and wind and could enjoy the plates of food I provided in a dry place.

And then the first real tragedy struck: Mami came down with feline distemper, a common disease among young cats. Since I had never seen a cat afflicted with this terrible disease before, I didn't really understand what was happening when Mami didn't leave the house he had been sleeping in for over a day and a half. When he stayed in the house on the afternoon of the second day, I started to worry. I went over to him, took him out, and immediately saw that he was grievously ill; his eyes were swollen, he was feverish, and he was suffering from a runny nose or the feline equivalent of one. I gently cradled him in my arms and took him inside the house with me.

I immediately called my friend the veterinarian. Mami was very weak and I could hold him in my arms while the vet examined him at my home. He said that Mami probably had both feline distemper and pneumonia and immediately gave him a serious shot of antibiotics.

It was as if Mami had been struck by a bolt of lightning. He jumped out of my arms and ran away as fast as he could. He didn't just run—he leaped like a tiger from the living room into the garden, and from the garden over the fence out into the street. I was filled with despair. I was sure that this was the end of Mami. The veterinarian made it perfectly clear that if Mami didn't get antibiotics in his food, he would die. But a cat is a smart animal. Since Mami probably felt better after the massive injection, he understood that he would be better off returning to the garden, and that's just what he did. Though Mami went straight to his cat house, he did start eating the medicine along with the appetizing food I provided, and so this time, at least, he recovered.

Since there were no other cats around these kittens, the difficult, contagious season passed and all four kittens were in the clear. Still, now that the veterinarian had explained it to me, I was now aware that the kittens could contract feline distemper even when they were older. But since I couldn't succeed in getting them vaccinated, there was nothing to do but hope they escaped infection.

Kitsushi started appearing in the garden once every few days. She would watch the kittens, but she no longer licked them. She even chased them away angrily when they came close to her. It was clear that as far as she was concerned their relationship had permanently entered a new phase. She had spent a few months with her kittens, and now they had to go out into the world and build their own lives. But what about her?

With time, Kitsushi went into heat again. But a strange thing happened—instead of mating with a group of cats, or at least with a few cats, she chased them all away. I understood the reason when one gray autumn day an enormous, rather mature cat appeared in the garden. It turned out that he was Kitsushi's regular mate. Kitsushi was shy and didn't couple with him in public, but judging from the sounds I heard at night, I guessed I was eavesdropping on a great love affair. During the four years that Kitsushi continued to visit me with her kittens, she was accompanied by the enormous cat, whom I named Geezer and who ended up becoming the first leader of my community of cats.

Geezer

Geezer was just as special a cat as Kitsushi was. She was a queen and he was an emperor. Geezer even babysat the kittens from time to time, and sometimes he would play with them—a rare thing for a tomcat. As for me, he accepted me only as his tenant and never as his landlady. His paternal attitude toward me was evident to all.

Let's return to our feline foursome, which by that time had grown up and become sexually mature. Nimroosh and Shufa had gotten pregnant and become mothers.

Nimroosh was an average mother. About six weeks after she gave birth, she started leaving her kittens alone for many hours while she went to one of the gardens within her territory.

Nimroosh

When she returned to the garden, she would nurse and clean them, but it was clear that there was an enormous difference between her mothering skills Kitsushi's. Nimroosh never took her kittens on border patrol, nor did she play the educational games that Kitsushi so diligently practiced with her kittens every day. As a result, Nimroosh failed to transmit essential life skills to her kittens. With time she learned to become a more devoted mother, but she was never an affectionate mother.

Shufa

Shufa, on the other hand, was a fanatical mother. She had given birth in a nearby garden and used to run, as if possessed, to grab pieces of chicken from me and bring them to her growing kittens. But her strength wasn't up to the task. I tried to help her as much as I could, but it wasn't enough. Shufa was small, and I guess the goal she had set for herself—raising her kittens properly—came at the expense of her health. One bright day she disappeared and left the kittens in the nearby garden.

The last time I saw her she was holding a large piece of chicken that I had given her in her mouth, and she was jumping over the fence to the garden where her kittens waited in order to give them the gift. I have no doubt that something must have happened to her since Shufa would never have abandoned her kittens. Perhaps she was run over, or perhaps she got sick and went to a secluded place to die.

Meanwhile, Darky became a very large cat and wanted to fight for the leadership of the community. The first fight occurred, and Geezer, who was in fact the leader, won during the initial stage of the battle cries. A fight between male cats begins with a war of sounds; each cat displays his vocal ability, which is probably an expression of his prowess. The battle can be decided at this stage. If it isn't, the cats then move on to the next, more physical stage.

Darky

After his defeat, Darky decided that his place wasn't with us and he left to find himself another territory where he could lead. Given his rare courage, his size, and his strength, I very much hope that he was successful. In any case, he never came back to visit us.

Mami, on the other hand, grew up to be a medium-sized cat and we grew even closer. He accepted Geezer's leadership and remained in the garden as part of Geezer's "warm-up act." A warm-up act is I what I call the cats that hang around the leader, mainly young males. They would court a female in heat until they wore her down. Then Geezer would appear and quickly succeed in mating with her.

During March, a month during which most feline females are in heat, Mami was preoccupied with love. He hardly appeared for meals, and one night he returned utterly exhausted. I very gently placed him on a warm bed inside a cat house and tried to get him to eat and drink, but without success. We went to the veterinarian and Mami was hospitalized. Despite the dedicated care that he received, he died from a serious case of pneumonia. I grieved for Mami for many days. This was the first time that I mourned one of my street cats.

In Mami's absence I was left with Kitsushi, Geezer, and their daughter Nimroosh from the first generation of kittens. Naturally, though, there were new additions: Nimroosh's six striped kittens, four of which survived. Two of Shufa's kittens, which I'd found in a nearby garden, also joined the community in my garden—one was gray, the other a tabby.

But the most significant thing that happened was the appearance of a completely new female cat from another family. She looked very different; she was mainly white and had large black and brown patches in a leopard pattern. Her tail was very thin but her face was beautiful, large, and intelligent. I called her Beauty.

Beauty

At first I called Nimroosh's kittens by numbers, since I couldn't quite tell them apart. Like their mother, they were very shy and no less timid, and they never let me touch them. During the following months, two kittens remained: a female that I named Big Mama, and a male that kept the original number I had given him, Number Four. From Shufa's litter, which had included two males, no kitten remained. They grew up quickly and left for other territories. The regular cats in the garden were therefore Nimroosh and Big Mama from the founding family, and Beauty, the mother of the second family.

Kitsushi disappeared for several months. She returned to the garden only after she had given birth to another litter. Geezer periodically came and went. During mating season, he appeared for longer periods of time and then stayed because of Kitsushi and her kittens.

Nimroosh lived in my garden for seven years. During that time, we formed a relationship based on trust and a wonderful friendship. Independent and individualistic as Nimroosh was, she never hesitated to come to me for help, whether it was a particularly bad runny nose or a sick kitten. Through the years I came to understand her language, and she mine. She gave birth twice a year, and in most cases at least four kittens survived. Some of the females stayed in my garden, while the males were all chased away. One sunny day, after her last kittens were sufficiently grown-up, Nimroosh disappeared and I never saw her again. Nothing out of the ordinary happened before she went away. A similar thing happened with other female cats around Nimroosh's age. I will return to this issue later, but this is one of the mysteries that surrounds cats for which I have no explanation.

Much later, as I was taking one of my walks around the Beit HaKerem neighborhood, I thought I saw Nimroosh. But this, of course, was just wishful thinking.

Big Mama became a wonderful mother, and as the years passed, she learned to accept my affection and care with love. I have no doubt that we understood each other. She always gave birth outside the garden, and I never knew where. Two months after giving birth, she would bring her kittens with her for meals and gradually teach them to stay in the garden when she went away. She was the second most prolific breeder in the garden after Beauty, giving birth to nearly half the cats in the neighborhood. She lived in my garden for nine years, and then, probably exhausted from all the births, she died in her bed.

As time passed and the number of cats in the garden increased, additional cats arrived off the street. I will tell some of their stories, like Nonny, Darky, Sasha, Shushka, Toto, and Turquoise. I'll also tell of some of the cats that were born in my garden.

I have chosen to write about those cats whose lives and characters were special and different in some way. However, these cats are representative of street cats in general, wherever they are.

At the time the community started I had no one to consult about various everyday problems. None of my neighbors was a cat lover. They were neutral at best and mostly hostile. Luckily I discovered that a woman who lived nearby, Naomi Zabar was her name, also fed cats and provided a place for them to sleep. However, her garden was far from the street and not many cats found their way to her place. The beauty was that Naomi became a close friend in everything concerning cats. This made me feel less alone and we discussed many of the problems I encountered over the years and she was a real help.

Chapter 3: Courageous Cats

Kitsushi brought me her second litter one cold and rainy winter day. The heroine of this tale is Fluffy, an extraordinary cat with a difficult life ahead of her. What happened to Fluffy caused me much anguish and guilt.

On these harsh winter days, having thoroughly bundled up against the cold, I went out to the cat houses to feed the cats (there were already several houses), when suddenly I saw Kitsushi, soaked to the bone, looking gaunt and exhausted. There were no kittens in sight. I ran back into the house and prepared a special plate. I took it out to Kitsushi and she ate the food slowly but with a good appetite. Later in the afternoon, I went out in the pouring rain again to serve dinner. I saw Kitsushi lying inside one of the cat houses underneath several gray and black fur balls. I couldn't exactly see what they looked like or even tell how many there were. I carefully placed a special plate next to the cat house and went back inside.

The next morning, the sun was shining, as it usually does during the winter in Jerusalem, and I could see that Kitsushi had arrived with four kittens. Two of them seemed to be made of Angora wool. One was so beautiful that it took my breath away. As I would later learn, this kitten was a female, which is how I will refer to her from now on, though at the time I had no inkling of her gender. I called her Fluffy after the fur ball she resembled. The other three kittens were also beautiful, though they were small and weak.

Fluffy: The Courageous Fur Ball

Fluffy's story is a tale of courage and inspiration the likes of which are usually only ascribed to people who have bravely faced traumatic experiences.

Fluffy

Once Kitsushi's woolly kittens were four months old, Kitsushi disappeared from the garden, as was her custom. Geezer, who had spent a significant part of those four months with Kitsushi and her kittens, vanished after her. The kittens stayed with me. Fluffy's beauty set her apart from the rest, as did her intelligence and resourcefulness. Even as a kitten, she already displayed leadership skills. Her siblings and the other cats, including some of the bigger ones, showed her respect and always let her eat first. It's important to know that the feeding order among cats reflects the community's internal hierarchy.

A hierarchy is established even when several families are involved. When Kitsushi and Geezer were in the garden, no cat dared approach the food before they ate. It was clear that Geezer was the ruler of the small community that lived and fed in my garden and that Kitsushi was the queen.

After these two disappeared, Fluffy took their place despite her youth. If one of the cats misbehaved, attempted to snatch food from another cat, cut in line, or invaded an overpopulated cat house, Fluffy would ensure that order was restored. One look from her sufficed to bend the cats to her will.

During that time, Nonny (there's more to tell about him, as he was to become the leader after Geezer) was but a two-month-old kitten and he obeyed Fluffy as well.

As time passed, Fluffy began exploring outside the garden, her walks becoming progressively longer and her absences lasting several days at times. However, after a certain five-day outing, I began to feel uneasy. This was too long an absence.

I set out to search for her, but to no avail. Fluffy wasn't in any of the neighborhood gardens. This is a good time to give a brief description of our little home. The garden, which I've already described, is located at the back of the house and is accessible by a door from the living room. The cats lived in the spacious garden, where their cat houses were located. They could access the garden by jumping over the surrounding fence. Near the front door of our home is another little garden. Four steps lead up to the front door from a path that connects our house with some others and leads out to the main road.

The cats tended to walk across the front path, but they didn't receive their food near the front door, with the exception of Beauty, her eldest daughter Colomina, and their kittens. And apart from Pishoosh—whose tale will soon follow and whom we found in the woodshed under the stairs—no cat ever hid in front of the house.

One afternoon, already worried about Fluffy's fate, I exited the house on my way to work at the university. I didn't see anything out of the ordinary, but a strange sound, like something dragging, caught my attention. I looked to the right, to the left, and then nearly fainted. To the left, on the path connecting our house with the neighboring ones, laid Fluffy. As I approached her, I saw that she wasn't lying down but was slowly dragging her whole body forward with her front legs. I immediately realized that Fluffy had been in a terrible accident, and her hind legs—if not the whole rear part of her body—were now paralyzed. Naturally I ran to her, determined to pick her up, bring her inside, take her to the veterinarian, and then keep her in the house if necessary. But Fluffy wouldn't let me get too close. She emitted a terrible hiss, opened her mouth threateningly, and it became clear that she had no intention of letting me touch her. Having quickly considered the situation, I returned home, prepared food and water, came out again, and placed them in front of Fluffy. I stood about two meters away from her, and she ate and drank slowly but thoroughly. Then she miraculously managed to turn her body around and dragged herself back along the path until she disappeared.

For several hours afterward I was in shock, crying. I was certain that this was the end of Fluffy. How would she be able to drag herself on rainy days to be fed? I didn't know where she was hiding, since the moment she heard me following her she stopped dragging herself. Only when she was sure that I wasn't looking did she continue moving until she disappeared.

During that first encounter with the crippled and emaciated Fluffy, I didn't see her display any sign of fear, anxiety, or despair; she was full of determination and courage, as evidenced by her conduct.

And so for a month, every afternoon at exactly the same time, I came out to the front of the house and the paralyzed Fluffy was waiting there for me and the food. She ate, and I made sure that she was not disturbed. Then she went away. As time passed, I noticed that she was dragging herself a little faster. I became hopeful. *Such courage and determination must bear fruit*, I thought. I had heard and read of cats recovering from horrific injuries, but I never imagined when I first saw Fluffy that she would be able to jump or walk on all four legs again. I hoped that with shelter against the wind and rain, her strength would hold up and she would be able to come to me every day to eat.

I never for a second thought that Fluffy would be able to make it into the back garden. To get into the garden the cats had to jump over a fence, though there was one spot where the fence was lower to allow kittens to come and go.

Fluffy's self-administered physiotherapy started to show results; not only could she haul herself faster than before, but it seemed to me that she was also moving the rear part of her body and hind legs a little, though not in any sort of coordinated way.

Two months went by and spring arrived. One morning I went out to the garden and to my surprise found myself facing Fluffy. She was sitting there in a slightly odd position, looking at me with eyes that demanded food. She had somehow managed to jump over the fence. She sat near one of the cat houses, which immediately emptied of its occupants, and waited for me and the food.

From up close I could finally see the severity of her injuries: her pelvic area and hind legs were paralyzed and probably fractured. She had no control over her bodily functions and I lovingly cleaned up after her several times a day using a damp cloth to clean her and another big cloth to clean the floor.

I began sleeping better at night knowing that Fluffy was in the garden, safe in a cat house. I didn't know to what extent she would recover from her injuries. My veterinarian friend, who came at my request and who had extensive experience treating cats, only managed to see her from afar. He later said that her recovery was nothing short of miraculous. I replied that Fluffy was a real hero. While a miracle might have played a part in her recovery, what got her through were mainly her strong character, rigorous discipline, and incredible willpower.

According to the veterinarian, Fluffy would never be able to lead a normal cat's life—she would remain paralyzed and be forced to stay in the garden. It goes without saying that he thought she would never go into heat, mate, or give birth. Though usually pessimistic, I told the veterinarian that given the extent of Fluffy's recovery, I would not be surprised if her condition improved even further. He was skeptical.

As the days and weeks passed, Fluffy's condition improved. Sometimes I would see her from afar, doing her physiotherapy. She would perform strange exercises that involved moving the rear part of her body and hind legs. It looked as if she knew what physiotherapy was, as in the beginning she made only very small movements, and when she felt that she was a little stronger she made bigger movements. A very slow process but a successful one.

Her perseverance bore fruit.

After a couple of months, Fluffy could control her bodily functions and stand on four legs. She began walking instead of dragging herself around. Though she moved stiffly and with a strange gait, she actually walked! And then one day I saw her jump over the garden fence. That was the day when I knew Fluffy would lead an almost normal life.

Fluffy never did get to live to a ripe old age. This, as we shall see, was my fault. It was certainly not due to any lack of motivation, iron willpower, intelligence, or determination on Fluffy's part. All these she had in abundance.

Once again Fluffy became the leader of the community. Throughout her rehabilitation, the other cats kept their distance and never disturbed her when she fed or exercised. No cat dared approach her. The only cat with whom she had some kind of contact was one of her brothers, a formerly small and weak kitten that had managed to survive. In time, and once Fluffy regained control of her bodily functions, her brother joined her in the cat house and would engage her in games that also served as therapy.

I spent much time watching Fluffy, all the while thinking how I wished I had her character. I might not be Fluffy's exact opposite, but there is much that I could learn from her willpower, patience, determination, perseverance, and optimism.

When summer came Fluffy behaved just like a normal cat. Apart from her gait, which was a little peculiar, there was nothing out of the ordinary that a stranger would have noticed.

And then Fluffy went into heat. This is how nature usually announces the return of health. I have learned that when a cat is sick, she does not go into estrus. For me this served as a red flag. During the previous mating season, when Fluffy was still recuperating, she was never in heat.

Yet Fluffy's pelvic injury made it impossible for her to mate. From the second-floor balcony, I witnessed futile nightly attempts at coupling. I was sorry for her, but I was also relieved, for I feared that even a partly paralyzed pelvis would prevent Fluffy from giving birth. It was clear to me that if her health improved further by the following mating season and she managed to get pregnant, her life would be in danger.

The reader may ask why I didn't spay Fluffy. This is a good question and the answer is simple. Just as Fluffy refused to let me touch her right after the accident, I knew she would not let me catch her and take her to the veterinarian. I consulted my veterinarian friend and he suggested that I put a sleeping pill in her food to make it easier to get her into the cage. I did as he suggested, but whenever I drugged her food Fluffy wouldn't touch it.

I also called a cat catcher, who brought a sophisticated trap into which I placed a salmon delicacy, but to no avail. No other cat dared enter the trap before Fluffy, as she was always granted the right to go first, but Fluffy instinctively knew this was a trap. She sniffed the salmon from afar but did not enter the trap. I finally gave up attempting to catch Fluffy and have her spayed; I simply hoped that she wouldn't get pregnant.

But as usual, life is unpredictable. After another year passed uneventfully, and when I finally stopped worrying about what would happen if Fluffy did manage to mate and get pregnant, I began noticing changes in Fluffy's body. She was pregnant!

I decided to try to find an excellent cat catcher who, despite the cruelty of the practice, might be able to snare her with a rope. I felt that Fluffy wouldn't survive the birth.

And this is one of the great sins that I carry with me to this day. I'd made the decision to call in this special cat catcher, but because of the difficulties involved, I kept putting it off, especially because according to our calculations Fluffy wasn't due for a while yet.

Because of my decision to delay and our miscalculations, my worst fears came true. Fluffy disappeared for about a week. I had an ominous feeling. I knew even before I saw her body that Fluffy had died in labor. On the eighth day after her disappearance, I meticulously searched our garden and the two adjacent gardens. After several hours, I found Fluffy's body. She had failed to give birth and the kittens had died inside her.

This was extremely traumatic for me. I believed then, as I believe now, that I was responsible for Fluffy's death. There were extenuating circumstances; the veterinarian who saw Fluffy during one of his house calls said that he had been mistaken and that Fluffy had a good chance of surviving the birth, and it seemed that Fluffy had gone into labor at least two weeks before her due date. Still, as far as I was concerned, what ultimately counted was the end result: Fluffy died and I could have prevented it. The guilt that has since plagued me has made me even more sensitive to the plight of street cats.

Sasha: The Brave Cat

Sasha's tale is similar to Fluffy's. She was a long-haired gray and white cat with large round eyes that lived in the garden across the street. Sasha wasn't one of my garden cats in the sense that she didn't live, play, or give birth in my garden, nor did she bring her kittens there. Sasha was simply a regular participant at mealtimes. One Saturday evening I went out into the garden on my way to visit friends, when all of a sudden I saw Sasha sprawled on the sidewalk near the road. I ran over to her and could immediately see that she had been run over. I called my veterinarian friend but he said he wasn't able to come because he was entertaining guests. I couldn't reach any other veterinarian and the responsibility of caring for Sasha fell on me alone.

Thinking of Fluffy, I remembered that cats have a remarkable ability to recuperate by themselves even from the most severe injuries. I examined Sasha, who let me touch her for a minute and then immediately started crawling away from me while emitting threatening sounds. I saw that her hind legs and pelvis were injured like Fluffy, but even though I wasn't a vet I thought that Sasha's injuries seemed less severe, though they were still bad enough.

I brought her nutritious food and after she ate, I tried to pick her up and bring her to one of the cat houses in the garden. But with unbelievable speed, she dragged herself across the road and disappeared into a large garden.

Sasha

Sasha behaved very much as Fluffy had. Every evening as darkness fell, Sasha appeared on the sidewalk, as if ashamed to be seen in her condition, and I would come out with a plate of food. I always stood next to her until she finished and watched her quickly drag herself across the road, which wasn't busy around that time, to the garden across the street.

Her condition steadily improved from one week to the next, and after three months she was herself again. For a long time afterward—

almost two years—Sasha continued to come and eat in my garden, into which she could now jump freely. But she never became a member of my feline community. Nature was kind to Sasha and she managed to get through four mating seasons without ever getting pregnant.

I don't know exactly when it happened, but I noticed that Sasha's appearances at mealtimes became less and less frequent. Finally she stopped coming over altogether and disappeared from my garden. I searched for her in the garden across the street, but without success. Sasha simply left us.

Sasha's disappearance is linked to a mystery that I've already mentioned: the disappearance of mature and healthy female cats. This is one mystery in the lives of cats that I have yet to unravel.

I have learned that when male cats reach sexual maturity, if they are not particularly big or strong, they tend to accept the authority of the tribe leader. If they are big and strong and aspire to challenge the leader, he in turn views them as a threat and violently drives them out of his territory. And so they disappear. Some of the older, sick cats also tend to vanish, particularly those cats afflicted with a disease called feline AIDS. They tend to embark on their final journey by themselves, preferring to die alone. (Feline AIDS is not contagious to humans.) Only rarely did sick male cats that had left the garden in their youth return to me to die. However, cats that lived in my garden for years, especially females, also died in the garden, lying in their cat houses. But why a healthy female cat would disappear—that I have never understood.

As for Sasha, I hope she found a better garden. I haven't seen her since the day she disappeared. Sasha was just as brave as Fluffy. But Fluffy recuperated in my garden and was the first cat to show me how a cat can overcome even the most horrific injuries by herself. This is why she remains the heroine of this chapter. I remember Fluffy just as she was, and Sasha I remember mainly her large round eyes.

Sophie: The Cat with Seven Souls

The third cat that was injured in an accident, though I don't believe a car was involved, was one of my favorites. Her name was Sophie. She somehow managed to get into a basement or climb up onto a roof, and in the process of either ascending or descending, she was seriously bruised.

Sophie was born, along with her brother Silver, to Big Mama, a most prolific feline whose kittens usually survived and matured magnificently. From the first day I laid eyes on them, Sophie and Silver were the most beautiful cats that I had ever seen after Fluffy. Sophie was white, and thin abstract drawings in yellow, orange, and grayish black decorated her coat as if painted there by an artist.

Sophie loved heights. Once she climbed all the way up a tree and was almost stuck there. I was starting to think about whom I could call on for help, when all of a sudden she rediscovered her courage and scaled her way back down the tree. Perhaps because she was a climber, I jumped to the conclusion that that's how Sophie must have been injured.

Sophie's unique character meant that the five years I had with her were tumultuous. When she was a year old, she would disappear for several days, only to return thinner than before but satisfied. Then the inevitable happened—for when a cat roams the streets freely, frequently crossing roads and climbing up to high places, it is bound to get into trouble. At the same time, I honestly can't say that I had a feeling that something would happen to Sophie, as she always seemed to me to be accident proof.

She would regularly disappear from the garden for a day or two, and as I walked down the street, I would sometimes see her sitting on a neighbor's roof or on the high branch of one of the trees in the neighborhood. This was what troubled me about her disappearances.

But when I came out to the yard that evening with the cats' supper, I heard a faint meow coming from somewhere near the cat pergola, but not from inside it. It was summer, and it was more pleasant out in the yard. I quickly divided the food among the cats and then went to investigate the source of the faint cry. I spotted her laying near the fence separating our house and the neighbor's. It was immediately clear to me that something was wrong; her posture wasn't normal for a cat. I approached Sophie, who only rarely let me touch her, but she didn't stop me when I came closer and very gently examined her with my hands.

That's how I discovered that she was seriously injured. Most of her body was covered in blood and one leg was bent awkwardly. I tried to ascertain the extent of her injuries and Sophie helped by trying to move. I could then see that one of her legs was broken, and the entire left side of her body was covered with bleeding wounds and scratches.

Taking her to the veterinarian was out of the question. The moment I approached her with a cage to try to get her inside, she gathered up what little strength she had left and started moving away. It was clear to me that she would run away—perhaps never to return—if I didn't put the cage away immediately. In the meantime, I could also see that she was very thin, which was another reason I assumed that she had been stuck on some roof or in some basement during her absence.

I had faith in Sophie. Fluffy taught me a lot about cats' endurance and their ability to heal.

Sophie lay in the same place for about a week, while I fed her and put antibiotics in her food. Her condition started to improve. At first she ate very little and mostly only drank water, but as the days passed, she grew stronger.

About a week later, I was getting out of my car when I saw Sophie crawling across the road under some parked cars. I didn't know what had happened—perhaps one of the cats had harassed her—but in any case, there she was. Despite a broken leg and multiple injuries, she managed to jump over the fence and was apparently trying to find a quiet spot.

I knelt near the cars and tried to coax Sophie out from under them, hoping she'd come back with me to the garden. Some kids passing by stopped near me. They were curious, as they had never seen an injured cat before. I asked them to leave and explained that I needed to be alone with the cat if there was any hope of getting her to come back home. I don't know how long I knelt there beside her. It felt like an eternity.

And then a remarkable thing happened: she let me lead her back to the yard. She didn't let me pick her up, of course. She simply crawled and limped beside me while I kept repeating, "Good Sophie. Good Sophie." And so we reached the low fence. She jumped over it with great difficulty, and I entered through the pergola. Slowly the two of us continued our journey until we reached her previous resting spot.

I shuddered to think what would have happened to Sophie if I hadn't managed to persuade her to return to the garden.

I learned my lesson and realized that I had to create a safer environment for Sophie to ensure that other cats in the garden couldn't harm her. By the way, it is quite rare for cats to harm an injured or sick cat, so it's possible that Sophie had left the yard simply because she was uncomfortable with the lack of privacy. I brought over an "open" cat house, which was just the bottom section of a cat house, and I padded it with newspapers and one of my old nightgowns. Around this bed I placed several cardboard boxes that partially hid the bed from the other cats.

It seemed that my knowledge of cat psychology helped identify the problem. What had really bothered Sophie was the lack of privacy. In any case, once I surrounded her bed with cardboard boxes and isolated her from the other cats, Sophie remained behind the cardboard boxes for over a month while she gradually healed. She walked around her bed and performed what I called physiotherapy in the space between her bed and the cardboard boxes. After a month, she left her corner and joined the other cats at mealtimes, later returning to her bed. After another two weeks, she left her corner for good.

Sophie never recovered completely and remained an invalid. Her paw was paralyzed and she learned to use the end of her foreleg as a paw. A stranger witnessing her gait would have thought that she was limping. She began leaving the yard and returned to her wayward ways, walking between the neighborhood gardens and occasionally attempting to climb, though I could see that she was more careful.

Sophie reached a new record when she once again climbed up onto the roof of the pergola. I have no idea how she managed to do it despite her handicap, but after several attempts, which probably took place at night, she succeeded, and one morning I was greeted by the sight of her coming down from the roof of the pergola. In fact, Sophie was nearly as active after the accident as she had been before it.

Sophie's injury did not stop her from getting pregnant a year later and giving birth to her first litter. I have no idea where she gave birth to the kittens, as it didn't happen in my garden. But when the kittens were barely two weeks old, she brought them to the yard.

Given her acute sense of interesting places to climb, while she was lying injured in her corner, Sophie must have found out that the wall of our house, which formed the back of the cat pergola, contained a treasure. That treasure was a basement, part of which was used to store plastic chairs. We used the chairs during the brief period when the large pergola was ours. With her paws, though one of them was crippled, Sophie managed to open the plastic basement door wide enough to bring her kittens inside through the opening. For about two months, the kittens grew up on the basement floor, and Sophie came in several times a day to feed and clean them.

Sophie never let me go down to the basement. All day long she sat on a high stool that stood near their new home. The moment I dared come close, she would jump toward me and emit warning growls. Knowing Sophie, I realized that I had to take her warnings seriously and I never tried to enter the basement.

But the basement was definitely not a good place to raise kittens—for two entire months they never saw daylight! When Sophie finally brought them out into the garden, the kittens were weak.

During the next month, I helped Sophie try to rescue them, but of her four kittens only one survived despite the food and medicine I lavished on them.

Courageous Cats

Sophie gave birth to her second litter in the garden belonging to our neighbor, a man who was indifferent and possibly hostile to cats. The neighbor never told me about it, and so I had no idea where Sophie's kittens were.

I saw Sophie every day when she came to eat and I had no premonition that something bad was going to happen. For some reason I didn't notice when Sophie missed the two last meals on a Thursday, which is why I was shocked and horrified on Friday afternoon when I saw the special municipal vehicle used for catching animals that residents reported as a health hazard. It was mostly cats that were reported.

I asked the driver which animal they were here to catch, and he told me that a cat had given birth in the garden of the resident of the fourth house on the street, and that so far they had managed to trap the mother and three kittens. Now they were trying to catch the rest of the litter.

I guessed that the cats he was talking about were Sophie and her kittens and I remembered that I hadn't seen Sophie during lunch and dinner the day before. I ran like a crazy person to the neighbor's house (I really did think that I was losing my mind), and I saw two kittens being trapped. Judging by their shape and color, they clearly belonged to Sophie. The city hall supervisor told me that Sophie had been caught the previous day. I inquired where Sophie and her kittens had been taken and found out that they were at the city pound. I ran home in a terrible crying fit and told my husband what had happened. Luckily he knew the municipal veterinarian and agreed to call him and ask that Sophie and the kittens not be killed, or worse, handed over to some laboratory for animal testing. It was settled that my husband would come to the pound on Sunday and pick up Sophie and the kittens.

I was restless throughout Friday and Saturday. I was afraid that the directive from the municipal veterinarian wouldn't arrive on time, because my husband spoke to the vet on Friday when the pound was closed. These two days were pure hell for me. Not since Fluffy's death had I been so traumatized by what was happening to the cats, even though there was never a shortage of tragedies in my cat community.

I calmed down only on Sunday afternoon when my husband returned home with Sophie and all her kittens. We moved them to the yard underneath the cat pergola. Sophie never brought this litter into the basement, but raised her kittens outside instead. As a result, all the kittens survived and grew into magnificent cats.

Sophie did bring her next litter down into the basement, and history repeated itself; only one kitten survived. Sophie abandoned her next litter, leaving one kitten with me when it was barely two weeks old. When all the kittens in her next litter died as well, Sophie must have concluded that she had no chance of continuing the species in our yard and that she had to find herself a new home. She slowly stopped acting like a member of the community and her absences increased. Two weeks later, I saw her eating from a trashcan on a nearby street. There was no doubt that she was preparing herself to search for a new territory with other males. The price she was willing to pay was high, and included, as I said, eating from trashcans after being accustomed to good and plentiful food for over five years.

I would like to write that Sophie said goodbye to me personally, but that would be a lie. She said her goodbyes to me as she did to her beloved roof, cat pergola, and yard. One day, after being away for a week, she appeared, ate a little, walked nervously around the yard, and then suddenly jumped over the fence and disappeared. In her way, she was saying goodbye to me and to her way of life during the past five years.

Three years have passed since Sophie left, and I never saw her again. I have a constant living reminder of Sophie. One of the two cats that now live in the closed pergola that was intended for people is Sophie's daughter. The cat's name is Pizzo and she is almost an exact replica of her mother. But Pizzo's story belongs in another chapter.

This chapter has been about courageous cats that fought for their lives and rebuilt them in the aftermath of horrific accidents. Though this chapter focuses not on the accidents that befall cats but rather on how they deal with them, I feel that I need to say something about accidents involving cars that injure so many cats.

For some reason, and I have seen this with my own eyes, many drivers tend to stop their cars when they see a dog crossing the road, but they do nothing when a cat is involved. It's as if they behave a cat is an insignificant creature and there is nothing wrong in running it over.

Street cats suffer terribly when involved in accidents with cars. On my street alone, many lethal accidents have occurred over the years, and many cats have been killed or gravely injured. Some of the cats hit by cars were born in my garden. The accidents always occur in a stretch of the road where drivers are supposed to slow down, as the road narrows significantly into more of a path than a regular street. But of course, the drivers at fault never slow down. I took the seriously injured cats to the veterinarian. It isn't difficult to pick up a seriously injured cat, wild as it might have been, put it into a cardboard box or a cat bed, and run with it to the vet—thankfully, for some time now we've had a veterinarian's office close by. In almost every case, the rescue attempt fails and the animal has to be put down.

Chapter 4: A Tale of Pishoosh, Shushka, and Friendship Between Cats

Chronologically, our story begins a year and a half after Kitsushi first arrived with her kittens.

One harsh winter day, we heard the fierce cries of a kitten. Nature equips kittens with particularly loud voices so their mothers can find them. We agreed that the cries were coming from the front of the house, from the entrance area. As mentioned earlier, a few stairs lead up to the entrance to our house, and we store firewood under these stairs. I went out in the pouring rain to look under the stairs, where I found a coal-black kitten, barely a month old, soaked to the bone and meowing ceaselessly. Naturally I decided to take him inside, dry him off, feed him, and then keep him in the house or move him to one of the warm cat houses in the garden. But the kitten wouldn't let me catch him. Every time I thought I had him, he quickly sprang away and slid between the logs.

I realized that I had no choice in the matter, so I brought out some food and set it on the firewood. The kitten was so suspicious that even though he must have been extremely hungry, he wouldn't approach the food as long as he thought that I was too close to him. Only when I went up the path did he come out of hiding. From above I peeked under the stairs and saw him eating more quickly and ravenously than I had ever seen a cat eat before, and then he disappeared back between the logs. He must have been so tired that he fell asleep. At any rate, he stopped meowing.

My husband, who heard the cries first, named the black kitten Pishoosh. Pishoosh was a cat unlike any I had ever seen before. From the moment he came to us, his independence and mature character were clear as day. He was a hardcore individualist, and unlike all the other male kittens, he never once let me stroke him for as long as he lived. He would show his love for us in other ways, such as rubbing up against our legs, emitting special sounds when he saw us, and other unique Pishoosh tricks.

Here I should stop for a moment and explain a particular arrangement concerning the house and the garden that didn't even last a year.

At one point, my husband and I decided to occasionally open the door connecting the living room and the garden and allow a few weak and sickly cats to come into the house. At that time, there were only ten or so cats in the garden. We placed two beds in the living room, not to be confused with the cat houses in the garden. The cat houses were made of plastic and lined with blankets, while the beds in the living room were made from soft cloth and were warm and fluffy. When one of our cats was feeling sick or wanted to indulge itself, the cat would overcome its fear of entering the house, tap on the living room door with its paw, we would open the door, and the cat would come in. The cat would usually stay in one of the beds in the living room for several hours, and then tap once again on the living room door to be let out.

During the summer, we would often keep the door to the garden open for several hours each day.

One thing readers should know is that nothing makes a street cat panic as much as entering a closed space like a living room. The cat will literally start climbing the walls from fear that there is no way out. The panic is so strong that even when the exit door is shown to the cat, tit cannot see it and continues running amok. This is a potentially dangerous situation, for during such panic attacks the cat can bang its head against the wall and even the ceiling several times.

Only a select few street cats ever dare enter a house, and they learn to do so gradually. The first time they come in they take a few steps, never getting too far from the door, and then quickly run back outside. Having learned the way out, they repeat this process several times, taking a few steps inside, and then quickly running back out. After practicing rapid entry and exit, they become more daring, walking farther into the room. Slowly, some street cats even learn to stay in a room for increasingly longer periods of time. These were the cats that came into our home and slept in the living room beds.

After Mami's first attempt, during which he seriously panicked, he never dared enter the living room again. Sasha also ran inside in such a frenzy her first time that she went all the way upstairs and jumped out a window onto the awning. I had to call the fire department to get her down.

Unlike these and most other cats, Pishoosh loved to come into the living room right from the start, exploring the place for smells and curling up in one of the beds. He started doing this when he was two months old after he left his firewood sanctuary at the front of the house and moved into one of the cat houses in the garden. He would enter the house from the garden and after a pleasant nap, if the door was open,

Pishoosh would return by himself to the garden. When the door was closed he would come to us and emit a special sound that meant, "I want out."

One clear day at the end of winter Pishoosh appeared in the garden accompanied by a five- or six-month-old cat, the same age as Pishoosh. His coat was gray and white. Where the stranger came from, we never learned, but it was clear that Pishoosh met this cat during one of his patrols of his territory (meaning the gardens in the territory belonging to my community of street cats), and the two became friends. Perhaps Pishoosh saw that the gray and white cat lived in worse conditions than he did. He probably wanted to show the cat his own living conditions, and so he brought him to the garden. At dusk, Pishoosh tapped on the living room door and when I opened it I saw that he was pushing the gray and white cat forward. His friend entered the living room and Pishoosh proceeded to walk in front of, alongside, and behind the newcomer, showing him all the wonders of the place. Eventually Pishoosh brought his friend to the bed where he used to nap, and they both settled down on it and nodded off together.

Pishoosh

From that day on, their daily visits became routine: every day at exactly the same time Pishoosh would tap on the living room door and he and Shushka (this was my name for the gray and white cat) would come in, explore the place, and take a nap. At that time, Shushka never dared tap on the living room door by himself and only came in with Pishoosh.

As I've mentioned before, wherever cats roam the streets, there are dangers and accidents. But knowing this doesn't provide any sort of emotional protection. To this day I still haven't managed to come to terms with the fact that accidents happen, and whenever a cat is injured I feel horrible.

One day, at the usual time, Pishoosh tapped on the door and came into the house, followed by Shushka, who was limping badly. Shushka wasn't himself. One of his legs was broken and it was dangling in the air pitifully. After both of them tried to get into the bed as Shushka emitted cries of distress, I called the veterinarian. I thought that getting Shushka into a cage would be an ordeal, but it turned out that Shushka had well-developed instincts and probably realized that I had his best interests at heart. He walked into the cage by himself, dragging his injured leg. I brought him to the veterinarian, who decided that Shushka needed to have a pin surgically inserted to reconnect the bones in his leg.

Shushka

During the three days Shushka was at the vet, Pishoosh was grief-stricken. It became so bad that on the second evening Pishoosh refused to go out into the garden and remained curled up in his bed. Luckily I had a litter box inside the house just in case. I showed Pishoosh the box and he immediately got the hang of it. He did his business there and returned to the bed. In the morning, when we got up, we found him asleep, while the litter box contained new evidence that he had used it during the night. And so Pishoosh stayed inside the house—he even ate his food in the living room—until Shushka returned.

When I brought Shushka inside in his cage and set him free in the living room, there was no end to the joy those two cats displayed! If readers have never seen a reunion like theirs, it's one of the most loving things to behold. Pishoosh licked Shushka constantly and danced around him making soft noises, and Shushka licked him back and responded with his own soft sounds. It was clear that Shushka needed to stay indoors to recuperate and receive treatment. I wondered how Fluffy and Sophie would have done if they had let me treat them inside the house. However, as I've mentioned, they absolutely refused even the slightest touch and clearly chose to recuperate outside by themselves. During the following days, Shushka remained indoors and Pishoosh spent most of his time beside him.

At the end of the week, Pishoosh tapped on the living room door and asked to be let out into the garden. Shushka immediately limped after him. After a short while, Shushka returned, while Pishoosh stayed outside. It seemed that as far as Pishoosh was concerned, the worst was over for Shushka. After a while, Shushka's leg improved and his walk almost returned to normal again.

Shushka's long period of recuperation, which was mostly spent indoors, practically turned him into a house cat. Now, in most cases, house cats are spayed or neutered. There are, however, two kinds of house cats. One is the house cat that lives indoors but frequently goes out for walks or amorous encounters in rare cases that the cat is not fixed. The second kind is the house cat that lives exclusively indoors and never goes out. Shushka was one of the former. There is no doubt that he would have found life without his outdoor excursions quite depressing, and by tapping on the door with his paw, he would demand to go out and come back in. Pishoosh, on the other hand, remained a street cat that simply wasn't afraid to spend some time inside an enclosed space. Though he sometimes spent an entire night with Shushka in the living room, the focus of his life was outside.

As I walked through the neighborhood on my way to the shopping center, I would often encounter Pishoosh and Shushka. They were inseparable and had developed a private dialect composed of body language and vocalization, which only they understood. Many neighbors noticed this interesting phenomenon and I received many varied comments on the pair of cats that always walked and played together.

Each morning and afternoon, Shushka would wait near the garden door for Pishoosh to arrive. Sometimes Shushka asked to go out into the garden by himself, but he rarely left the garden unless Pishoosh appeared, and then the pair's stroll around the neighborhood would begin.

Watching this pair was one of my favorite pastimes. I had read and heard about friendship between animals. But it is one thing to know something and quite another to witness it firsthand. It turns out that cats, who many regard as individualistic and egoistic animals, can become social and, in Pishoosh and Shushka's case, even empathic creatures under certain conditions. Friendship between two young males is one such case. I will tell about friendship between mothers later.

For some reason, I decided right from the start not to photograph the cats, perhaps because I don't like photos. But I do have one picture of Shushka sleeping on one of the couches in the living room, lying on his back with his tail hanging down. With a heavy heart I sometimes look at this photo, for Shushka's life, while beautiful and special, was also very short.

One afternoon, at around five o'clock, Shushka asked to be let out the front door. I opened the door and said, "Have a nice walk, Shushka. See you later." Pishoosh was already waiting at the corner and I could see both of them running toward one of the gardens.

By eight o'clock in the evening I was extremely worried. I went out into the garden but could find no trace of either Shushka or Pishoosh. I had a bad feeling and it only grew worse with time. Night had already fallen. I started searching for the pair in their favorite gardens, but to no avail.

I thought they might have decided to go out on a long walk or even change territories, but then I dismissed both options, for I knew that Shushka had become a house cat and that Pishoosh would never have tried to entice him to take a long walk or leave his territory. I assumed that long walks were still not a simple matter for Shushka.

There was nothing I could do but return home and wait. Every half hour I went out into the garden and to the front of the house, but there was no trace of the two cats. At midnight I went to sleep with a very heavy heart.

I got up at first light and went out into the garden, but there still wasn't any sign of Shushka or Pishoosh. They weren't by the front door either. I went back inside, had a cup of coffee, tried to swallow a slice of bread, and finally decided to go out, determined to find out what has happened.

I was astonished when I opened the front door and discovered Pishoosh lying on the porch looking miserable and devastated. I immediately realized that something had happened to Shushka and that Pishoosh had come to inform me. After I walked down the stairs, Pishoosh leaped in front of me and started walking. I decided to follow him. Pishoosh walked down the road to the right. I followed him and after passing two gardens, we arrived at another road. Pishoosh stopped on the side of the road, sniffing it and emitting strange sounds. I came closer and saw blood stains. Before I had time to think, I heard a voice calling out from one of the balconies, "Lady, if you had a gray and white cat, you should stop looking for him. He was run over right here yesterday evening and this morning the municipal truck took away his body." I burst into uncontrollable tears and started running back home. Pishoosh stayed where Shushka had died.

Pishoosh and I mourned Shushka for a long time. I think that Pishoosh kept searching for Shushka until the day he passed away, never really accepting the fact that Shushka was dead.

Three years after Shushka passed away, Pishoosh went out on a long walk. When almost two weeks had passed without sight of him, I began to think that Pishoosh had moved to a new territory or that he might have fallen ill without my noticing and went to die in a secluded place.

But that's not what happened. One morning I went out to the cat pergola (by that time there was no longer a garden, but rather a pergola for humans, a cat pergola, and the yard) and there I saw Pishoosh, asleep in one of the cat beds. At first I thought that he was resting after a long and arduous journey, but something about his appearance was off. I approached the bed and called his name. Pishoosh awoke and sat up with great difficulty. That's when I saw that all the skin on his left cheek was missing, as was part of the skin on the left side of his body. The sight was horrific. A third of his body was bleeding and bare.

I called the veterinarian and asked him what I should do. I was afraid that Pishoosh wouldn't let the vet come near him, but when the veterinarian arrived, he managed to examine Pishoosh from a distance of about three feet. Pishoosh must have let him get so close because he was exhausted.

The veterinarian assumed, as I did, that Pishoosh had been in an accident that ripped off his skin, or it might have happened in a fight between males. In any case, treatment included antibiotics to prevent infection, good food, and, most important, plenty of rest.

Pishoosh's behavior was exemplary. He took the antibiotics that I mixed in his food, even though in the past when he had gotten sick he could immediately sense the medicine and avoided his food, eating from another cat's plate instead. This time it seemed he understood that the medicine was crucial for his health. As for rest, Pishoosh was so beaten up that he hardly left his bed for nearly three weeks. He spent most of that time sleeping.

Little by little, Pishoosh's wounds began to heal and new skin and hair began to form. Pishoosh spent about four months in the cat pergola and in the yard without venturing outside this area. As he grew stronger, a new problem arose: Pishoosh was quite the male, though physically he was not very big. As long as it wasn't mating season and Pishoosh stayed in his bed, everything was fine. Nonny was now the leader and his attitude toward the convalescing Pishoosh was sympathetic. Even when Pishoosh was well on the road to recovery and started taking more walks around the yard near the females, Nonny was forgiving and did not attempt to drive him away. I was sure, given their relationship, that when Pishoosh finally got his health back, Nonny would let him continue living in the garden as long as Pishoosh did not challenge Nonny's leadership. I didn't believe that Pishoosh would take on Nonny. I therefore hoped that the two of them would find a way to coexist. At that point Nonny had been leading the community for only two years, so I didn't expect any changes.

But as in the human world, so in the world of cats there is no end to unexpected and unpredictable events. One day when Pishoosh was already well on his way to recovery and Nonny had just gotten back from one of his long walks, a gray cat named Stripy—who had been born in the garden and of whom more will be told—decided to challenge Nonny's leadership. Stripy had been abandoned as a kitten by his mother, and though I raised him with love, he turned out to be a belligerent, power-loving adult cat.

All night long the cries of fighting male cats disturbed my sleep. I imagined that a fight was taking place between Stripy and Nonny. At first light I went out with great trepidation to see if Nonny was still in the yard, or if Stripy had managed to run him off after several fights.

Stripy

Since Nonny was my great love, more than anything I feared that he would be driven away from the yard forever and that I would never see him again. (Nonny's unique place in my life will be made clear in a later chapter.) When I went outside, for once not bringing any cat food with me, I saw Stripy sitting in the middle of the yard and Nonny was nowhere to be found. I was devastated. I was also concerned for the recuperating Pishoosh, as I had no doubt that he would also be driven away by Stripy.

I returned to our pergola. Utterly dejected, I began preparing food for the cats and then went out to feed them. Stripy came forward first and all the others waited. Overnight they had accepted his leadership without question. But after a careful survey of the yard, I saw that three females were missing. As for Pishoosh, he stayed near his bed and I brought him a specially prepared plate of food.

I went back inside the house and listened, hoping to hear Nonny tapping on the front door (after the pergola was built, only the front door of our house was accessible). I waited and waited until suddenly I heard distinct taps at the door. My heart was pounding as I ran to the door and opened it. Nonny stood outside, scratched and scruffy, but with his dignity intact. Behind him stood the three females that had left the yard.

I let Nonny inside as usual—over time Nonny had become both a house cat and street cat—and I assumed the three females outside just happened to be there. I gave Nonny food and water, cleaned his wounds, and left him on the first floor to rest.

I now had two male cats, Darky and Nonny, in one territory with Stripy. I did not know what would happen to them and the thought of living without Nonny in particular evoked such great sorrow so that I could hardly stand it.

There was nothing I could do. There is no way of driving off a male cat that has taken over a territory. I knew this not only from reading books, but also from experience with my community of cats.

Neutering Nonny and turning him exclusively into a house cat was an option. I seriously considered this path but ultimately decided against it. Nonny was a male in every sense of the word, and I didn't think it was my place to take away his manhood.

I was also concerned about Pishoosh's future, but less so. I hoped that since he posed no threat to Stripy in his condition, he would not be driven away from the yard and might even agree to swallow some of his pride and become one of the males that accompany the leader, that is, part of Stripy's "warm-up act."

When I came out of the house I saw the three females still waiting at the entrance, and I understood that they were waiting for me to feed them there.

Unfortunately the neighbors would make my life and the cats' lives a living hell if I left food in front of the house. I considered the matter and decided that I would bring out a single plate of food and stand next to the cats until they finished eating, and then immediately remove the plate. Like a thief, I furtively looked to my right at my neighbors' front doors and as soon as I saw the coast was clear I brought out a plate and blocked the sight the best I could. I waited until they finished eating and quickly removed all traces of the crime. It dawned on me that the three females had decided to link their fate to Nonny's and did not want to accept Stripy's leadership. I wondered how events would unfold.

After two days of the same routine, Nonny went outside—through the front door, of course—and instead of turning left as he usually did and jumping over the fence into the yard, he disappeared into the adjacent garden. After a few minutes the three female cats disappeared after him.

And so began the bifurcation of the community; the majority of the cats remained in the yard under Stripy's leadership, and a small minority followed Nonny into another garden where Stripy left them alone, though it was still within our territory. In this way Nonny got to stay in my house and remain a leader, though he had to make do with only a handful of subjects. Luckily the neighbors living near the garden to which the smaller part of my community had relocated were also cat lovers and didn't mind when brought food to the garden on a daily basis. And so Stripy became the leader behind the house, and Nonny the leader in front.

As for Pishoosh, he grew stronger every day and when he finally reached his full strength again, I realized that he would not back down. He would battle Stripy and, if he lost, he'd leave the yard and seek out a new territory for himself. And so it was. Pishoosh fought tooth and nail for over a week and when he finally lost (not by knockout, I think, but by points) he came to say goodbye. He rubbed up against my legs for a long time, gave me a look that said everything there was to say, and went on his way.

I was sure that I would never see Pishoosh again, but I was overjoyed to find out that I was wrong. Every few months Pishoosh would come to the house and tap on the front door, and just like in the good old days with Shushka, he would enter the living room, eat, drink, and sleep. If Nonny was in his usual place that day on the first floor, they would sniff each other, as if they were happy to be reunited and wished each other luck. Pishoosh would usually stay over for a day or so and then disappear again for a few months. This continued for four years until one day he left and never returned.

Pishoosh was and remains for me a symbol of the power of a strong personality. Against all odds— he was abandoned at a very young age on a bitterly cold winter night—he managed to bring us to him, to grow up and develop courage and pride, and to lead a life full of adventure and intrigue. Even after his horrible accident, he never lost an ounce of courage or became depressed. In this he was like Fluffy; both of them were great warriors.

I'm not sure if Pishoosh is dead. He would be thirteen now and may very well still be alive somewhere in the neighborhood. I wouldn't be surprised if this turned out to be the case, for Pishoosh the fighter was a true survivor. Perhaps in his old age Pishoosh has found a soul mate like his Shushka.

Chapter 5:
Motherhood and Joint Motherhood

There were many births in my community of cats during the years the cats lived with me. Neutering and spaying mostly began seven years ago, once the practice became accepted and available. I chose a veterinary hospital in the center of the country near Tel Aviv. A special car dispatched from the hospital would arrive with a cat catcher. The catcher would work for about an hour and a half and then put the cats in the car, each in a separate cage. The cats were taken to the hospital and were returned the next day after being neutered or spayed and receiving all necessary vaccinations.

Though I've done it many times over the years, the entire operation makes me shudder anew each time. But when I think about the alternative, I am grateful for the program.

When I write "alternative," I'm referring to threats such as when a neighbor told me that if I didn't transfer at least half of the cats in my community to a different location, he would call the municipal animal catchers to destroy the cats. Since I knew that he was serious, I contacted someone who was a professional cat catcher who could relocate them. Before evening fell he arrived with his cages and traps and systematically caught half the cats in my garden.

That evening I was beside myself with grief. All I could do was ask him to catch entire families so they would have the company of their kin and friends in their new location. I felt that this operation, the result of a neighbor's threat, should not have taken place. Even when the cats were already in the car, I begged the neighbor, tears streaming down my face, not to demand these cats be transferred, as they were accustomed to me and my garden. To my great sorrow, the neighbor refused. I could only try and take comfort in the hope that the cats were relocated to a good neighborhood in Jerusalem where there weren't many cats.

To this day I still haven't made my peace with this despicable relocation, and I agonize over it.

When the number of cats in my community significantly increased once more, I didn't wait for the neighbor's threats. I swore that I would never again take part in what was in my opinion an unjustified transfer. With the help of several societies for the welfare of cats I found adoptive families, as well as a kibbutz that took in several cats. This time I was a bit calmer.

The cat overpopulation problem was the result of the fact that during the first seven years of my community, no spaying and neutering program existed; there were only festivals of love twice a year with new litters arriving six weeks later. Cats have two mating seasons a year, so new births occur almost simultaneously. Sometimes a female that has lost her kittens comes into heat out of season, and then there is a lone litter.

During the first seven years of birthing seasons, before the pergolas were built, the cats could come up to the door leading to the living room. Their houses, located in the clearing in the middle of the garden, were quite close to the living room. Sometimes during the birthing seasons I would even place two houses right near the living room door to make it easier for me to take care of the mothers and kittens.

During the first two years nothing unusual happened. Every female cat gave birth to her kittens, usually in the garden itself. Sometimes, however, cats would give birth in an unknown location and after a few days or weeks they'd return with their kittens. Mothers would bring the kittens one at a time, each kitten held in its mother's mouth.

In preparation for the births—this was when there were four or five births happening at once—I would pad the cat houses with newspapers instead of the usual blankets. This way the first time the mother left her kittens for a few minutes after she gave birth, which was usually after about a day and a half, I would remove the blood- and fluid-soaked newspapers and replace them with fresh ones. During the first month after the birth I would change the newspapers every two or three days. The number of newspapers required for this operation was enormous and the two daily newspapers I subscribed to did not suffice. I used to ask the neighbors to give me their old newspapers. To this day I think this is a very constructive use for discarded daily papers.

In any case, though the average size of a litter for cats is six kittens, oftentimes a kitten or two would die during the first couple of weeks, so more often than not only four kittens remained for the mother to raise. This was an arduous task for a street cat without a home or permanent feeding station. Two weeks after the birthing season, emaciated cats with prominent teats can be seen on the streets, and near trashcans, and it is obvious that they are nursing mothers. Luckily for my females, they had a house with a bed, the kittens, and me. With great curiosity I watched elongated creatures with eyes tightly closed emerged from Pizzo and slowly transform into the shape of cats.

The unlucky street cats can usually bear the burden of raising their kittens for no more than six weeks. Afterward they abandon the kittens and go elsewhere. At six weeks old, kittens can eat by themselves and even search for food alone, but because they are so small, almost all of them die. If one kitten survives from a street cat's litter, it's a success. That is why even before the neutering and spaying program began, the city wasn't overrun by cats, though there were more than there are now.

In our garden kittens grew up without any hassle and mothers took care of them for four months. This means that they nursed the kittens for three months, though as the kittens grew the number of nursing sessions per day decreased, and the kittens began eating more and more of the food I supplied.

At first I placed kitten food on a special plate, but soon enough they started approaching plates meant for other cats, not just their mother's, and eating with the bigger cats. It was easy to see how the transition from life among their mother and other kittens—at first their siblings, and later kittens from other litters as well—to eating with the adults made the kittens feel independent and important. The adult cats always made room for the little ones to eat.

During the first month, kittens tended to spend most of their time with their mother, and when they began to play it was usually with their mother's tail or with their siblings. As the weeks went by, I would see kittens from different litters approach one another and begin to make friends.

Friendships developed between kittens with different mothers, and some of them lasted for years. A kitten's first preference was still for its siblings, but little by little friends played a more prominent role in the kittens' lives.

Mothers clearly played the central role in kittens' lives until they reached four months old, sometimes older. Though kittens gradually nursed less and less, it was during this time that mothers guarded their kittens, groomed them, and taught them various cat skills. This was actually a very rare occurrence in the society of street cats. Usually even if a mother had pretty decent conditions—that is, food and a place to sleep—she left her kittens the moment they could feed themselves. But in our garden the kittens underwent extensive training, sometimes right up until the next time their mother went into heat, and at times even afterward.

What role nurture versus nature plays is something that unfortunately I still don't understand despite many years of observing street cats. To this day I still can't decide whether cats' hygienic practices are genetic or the results of learning through imitation.

Be that as it may, the moment kittens started strolling around the garden, they began relieving themselves just like the adults. It was hilarious and touching to see one of Pizzo's kitten digging in the earth at ferocious speed with his miniature forelegs and covering his business with sand.

Mothers also gathered their kittens together several times a day for a shared family experience, which could be a short nursing session, or a few games and a quick nap with the kittens laying one on top of the other. When the sun was shining, there were three or four piles in the garden consisting of a mother and her kittens, and by the color of each pile I could tell which family it was.

It is true that in the beginning most of the families in my garden were grayish white, black, and stripped, but over time as a few ginger and black and white males managed to infiltrate the community, ginger, tricolor, and black and white kittens began to appear. Sometimes the piles were very colorful indeed with all the multicolored offspring.

Most mothers, especially the more experienced ones, took their kittens on border patrol and from time to time a family would disappear for two days and return famished. I knew they had returned from an extensive exploration of their territory. As I've already mentioned, the border patrol was a mother's way of preparing her kittens to be independent.

Training kittens to be independent was a gradual process that required mothers to leave their kittens for increasingly longer periods of time. Some kittens naturally adapted to the hours and then days without their mother, and others looked a little scared. But at the end of the process all kittens began taking charge of their lives, as they understood the hard way that they no longer had a mother. Sometimes when their mother was near, they would approach her to receive a lick or a loving pat, but the mother's reaction was always aggressive and the kittens eventually realized that they now had sole responsibility for their lives.

Usually kittens would stay with their siblings and friends from other families until they reached sexual maturity. Male kittens in particular were friendly and sought the affection of siblings and friends. Females spent many hours by themselves, as if mentally preparing for the fact that very soon they would become mothers themselves. But there were also females who maintained relationships with a single sibling, often a male, or with a single friend from another family.

With the onset of sexual maturity and pregnancy, females behaved like adults in every way. More than once I contemplated how cruel nature was to enable seven-and eight-month- old female cats to get pregnant when their body was still too small and fragile for the experience.

Males, who also reached sexual maturity sometime between seven and ten months, were not necessarily driven away at this age by the leader of the community. Early on I learned that the leader teaches young males about the art of love—that is, to the young males he decided to keep around. As I've already described, the role of the young males who became part of what I called the "warm-up act" was to try and court a female in heat that was usually not interested in mating and eventually wear her down. Afterward, the leader would approach the female who was by then exhausted, and all he had to do was perform a short courtship and mate with her.

But before I continue with the subject of motherhood, let's address the question of whether fatherhood beyond the biological aspect is possible in the cat world.

During all the years I took care of cats, I only saw one male that remained loyal to one female above all others. His sexual escapades with other females were just sex, and it was always clear that his mate was the only one he cared about. This male, Geezer, was husband to only one female, Kitsushi, throughout his life. He also helped her after she gave birth and many times I would see him look after Kitsushi's kittens when she needed to take a few hours off or even half a day. (Given the incredible number of kittens she gave birth to, it is no wonder that she grew tired of raising them for four months at a time.) I also saw Geezer bring food in his mouth for the kittens, such as parts of a chicken he had found in the dumpster or a bird he had caught.

Apart from this cat, other males did not accept any parental responsibility, which obviously meant that kittens never knew which cat was their father. There may be logic to this, since kittens in one litter come from different fathers. So why should one father take responsibility for another's kittens? And yet I believe that Geezer's kittens grew with more confidence and better life skills because they had a big male cat around. What this father taught Kitsushi's kittens, I have no idea. To me it looked like a game of wrestling he played with them.

Let's return to mothers that are in fact responsible for raising and educating their young.

Events that occurred one spring in particular were an example of one of the most beautiful things I have ever witnessed in the cat community.

In April, four cats gave birth in the garden. Two of them, Bear and Mimi, were first-time mothers and took over the cat houses near the living room door. They had been friends since kittenhood and later shared the same cat house, took walks together, and continued playing with each other even while they were pregnant.

Bear

Mimi

Big Mama

Teddy

The other two mothers, Big Mama and Teddy, had given birth before. They occupied two of the cat houses in the garden. The births were successful and there were six beautiful kittens in each litter.

Perhaps because the weather was wonderful, food plentiful, and hygiene was good, all the kittens survived the second week. And then I saw that despite these ideal conditions, Bear began losing strength. She was having a difficult time nursing and grooming her six kittens. Bear wasn't particularly small, but perhaps because this was her first litter she might not have had enough milk or simply was not strong enough. In any case, Mimi, who had given birth in the adjacent cat house, saw that Bear was in trouble. Bear was white with black patches; Mimi was gray and white. Bear's kittens were white with black patches or black with white patches, and one kitten was a tabby; Mimi's kittens were a motley bunch. In short, distinguishing which kitten belonged to which mother was very easy.

And so it happened that I came to witness a touching scene. One day I saw Mimi sprawled on the ground, nursing not her own kittens, but Bear's. Bear was asleep. I went out to the garden with a book, sat on a patio chair, and waited to see what would happen to Mimi's kittens.

Mimi's kittens were sleeping in a heap, not a sound was to be heard, and so I assumed they were not hungry. I concluded that Mimi must have nursed them before taking care of Bear's kittens.

I spent several hours in the garden that day and the following days and saw how Mimi would occasionally nurse Bear's kittens, while Bear grew stronger day by day and the number of feedings she could manage each day increased as well.

Mimi not only nursed Bear's kittens, but she also groomed them properly and could often be found curled up with a dozen kittens.

Mimi must have understood the precise nature of Bear's plight—that she needed to sleep and gather her strength—and she knew exactly what needed to be done. This was also Mimi's first time giving birth, but nature seemed to have favored her with strength and milk.

Bear accepted the assistance Mimi provided as the natural order of things, and it was clear to me that if the situation had been reversed, Bear would be the one helping Mimi.

Slowly, Bear grew stronger and began nursing her own kittens. But then an interesting thing happened: gradually the dozen kittens stopped being the six belonging to Mimi and the six belonging to Bear. Instead, they became common kittens. The colors mixed together and the two mothers raised twelve kittens together.

I was sure that Mimi and Bear could no longer identify their own kittens. I was wrong. It turned out that at night Mimi and Bear would each sleep with her own litter. Incidentally, this indicated that the kittens themselves could distinguish between their core family and their extended family. The life of this extended family was the most beautiful thing I've ever seen.

This joint motherhood lasted for the four months during which Mimi and Bear continued to nurse, groom, and teach their kittens. After two months, they would alternate taking mini breaks, thus allowing themselves several hours off from the grueling task of raising kittens. The kittens themselves formed interesting friendships that last to this day.

This joint motherhood became the model for Mimi and Bear. The second time they gave birth, it was clear that they would be helping each other right from the start. This time it was actually Mimi who needed assistance, having caught a cold in the third week following the birth. And so it was Bear who took care of all the kittens this time while Mimi rested and recuperated.

Big Mama and Teddy were amazed at the sight of this joint motherhood. They sat and watched what was going on for hours and sometimes even missed a meal due to how absorbed they were in what was going on. They were sisters that maintained close ties. Their cat houses were close to each other and both gave birth in my garden rather than elsewhere. But here the traditional family structure was maintained: each mother took care of her own kittens, and while the kittens played together, each mother took responsibility solely for her own offspring.

It seems that what Big Mama and Teddy saw in Mimi and Bear's relationship must have impressed them or aroused their jealously and amazement. In any case, they adopted some of the behavioral patterns of joint motherhood that had been absent from their previous births.

The kittensitter role was created. Once their kittens were a month old, two mothers would take turns guarding both litters, and in this way they could take longer breaks from time to time. They also started grooming each other's kittens and when one of them taught her kittens new things— by playing what I would call educational games—she would call out in a special way to her sister's kittens and they would promptly join her. As the kittens grew older, the mothers became less and less concerned with maintaining the biological family framework and the friendships that formed were in the context of the extended family. The result was actually two extended families in the garden instead of four biological families. It was fascinating!

The two families lived side by side harmoniously, but no friendships formed between members of the two extended families.

When she was three years old, Teddy experienced an extremely difficult premature birth, and she bled extensively. She was so weak from the loss of blood that I encountered no resistance as I took her to the veterinarian. Her treatment also included spaying.

Teddy never gave birth again, but for the rest of her life she continued helping Big Mama raise her kittens. They also passed away a month apart when they were nine years old. Neither one managed to survive a particularly snowy, terrible Jerusalem winter. Despite the protection the cat houses provided, warm blankets, and a regular supply of food, both were already weak. In Big Mama's case, it was the result of numerous births, and in Teddy's case it seemed she had never fully recovered from the final difficult birth she had gone through. Both died in their sleep. Teddy entered her cat house in the evening and in the morning I found her lifeless. Following her death, Big Mama disappeared for several weeks. She returned gaunt and exhausted and after a few days, during which I tried to revive her, she also died in her cat house.

As for Mimi and Bear, both were relocated to another neighborhood during a terrible transfer. I was not told where they had been taken and so I don't know what happened to them. I find it hard to write about their transfer even now. In short, one of my neighbors could not stand that I was feeding such a large number of cats and he came with an ultimatum that either I found someone who would catch and relocate the cats to another neighborhood or he would take much more drastic measures. In the late nineties, there were no laws or regulations that protected street cats, so I had to comply and in the end almost half of my community was transferred. Years afterward I still had nightmares that they were sold to the laboratories at Hadassah Medical Center. These days nothing like this can happen thanks to laws and regulations safeguarding the rights of street cats, which center on a policy of trap, neuter, and return.

Today I employ the trap, neuter, and return method. The period of time back in the nineties—when the absence of professional help meant I could not trap cats and take them to be neutered or spayed— seems to me both romantic and problematic. Even today I keep asking myself what is better for a cat, to be healthy and live longer but be fixed, or to live a less healthy, shorter life and experience life fully as females and males. I think that if the cats could voice an opinion, they would choose the natural way.

The problem is that the solution of neutering and spaying is done mainly for the benefit of humans—to manage the number of cats on the streets—and less for the cats' quality of life, though there is no doubt that a street cat without a place to sleep or eat enjoys better health if he or she is fixed. But this practice is the end of motherhood and new generations.

I hope that one day a solution will be found that balances people's needs, the health of street cats, and the right of cats to live full and natural lives.

Special expressions of motherhood, both good and bad, naturally took place during those years in the garden, and later in the cat pergola and in the yard. Even today, despite the neutering and spaying program that I've initiated, a few males and females always remain uncaught.

It's interesting to see mothers' reactions to weak kittens. Mothers can usually identify weak kittens with low chances of survival and concentrate their efforts on their stronger offspring. When a kitten is sick, the mother usually does not tend to it, but rather leaves it alone, almost as if she has forgotten it exists. These abandoned kittens have no chance of surviving unless they are cared for by someone else.

I also experienced cases of sick kittens who were abandoned by their mothers that continued raising the stronger siblings in the garden or yard. I also had sickly kittens come to me from outside. In all these cases I was the one who took care of the kittens. Despite all my efforts, I was not always successful. I've already told the story of two abandoned kittens, Pishoosh and Shushka, and I will tell similar stories later.

Beauty's behavior toward her weak kittens was unlike most females (the story of Beauty and her daughter Colomina will follow in the next chapter.). Beauty would bring each of her sick kittens to my front door, which seemed to indicate that she wanted me to provide palliative care. She would not abandon a kitten, but rather stayed with me as I gave it special food and medication, and then she would take it back to where she and the other kittens lived. I never managed to discover that place. Beauty, as we will see, also adopted the abandoned kittens of other cats and nursed and raised them with her own.

Big Mama also never abandoned a sick kitten and would faithfully try to take care of it by herself. When she realized that a kitten was not improving, she would bring it to me in her mouth, place it near me, and meow in a special way.

During one winter birth, half of Big Mama's kittens got sick when they were about a month old. Because of the cold, I wasn't happy with them living in the garden, so I brought them inside sand tried to take care of them myself by following the veterinarian's advice. I saw that this time I couldn't manage it. Usually I could take care of sick kittens by following professional advice without having to bring the kittens to the vet, but this time I took all the kittens in for treatment. Several kittens survived.

Before I continue on the subject of motherhood, I want to clarify something about caring for cats. The best thing was to inoculate kittens at eight or nine weeks with the regular vaccinations against common cat diseases, including feline distemper, and then inoculate them again at twelve weeks. They should also receive the rabies vaccine at three to six months. However, as readers have seen, it was very difficult to catch kittens in time for these vaccinations to be effective.

An alternative method was to call a cat catcher from the veterinary hospital once a year, trap the cats, and bring them to the hospital where they received all necessary vaccinations. What made this option less than ideal was that some kittens didn't get vaccinated until they were already several months old, which left them exposed to infectious diseases when they were very young.

Besides vaccinations, the success of treating a cat depended first of all on how quickly the problem could be identified and how quickly the cat could be caught and taken to the vet. If the cat couldn't be caught, treatment depended solely on how accurately I could describe its condition to the vet.

As I've already said, when it came to adult cats, most of them couldn't be caught or put in a cage. I had to take care of them by myself, aided by the veterinarian's advice (for example, which antibiotics to give, if any). Only when their condition became so bad and they grew so weak that they couldn't resist did I manage to bring them to the veterinarian. Clearly, once things progressed that far, it was very difficult to save the cat.

Let's return to expressions of motherhood. One day one of Sophie's kittens climbed up to the roof of the pergola and couldn't get down. Sophie went up to the roof and tried to show him how to get down, but in vain. The kitten was too big for her to pick up in her mouth. I assumed that after numerous attempts to teach her kitten to climb down from the roof, Sophie understood that this was a lost cause and began meowing ceaselessly. These cries made me come outside at an unusual hour. Sophie then showed me that a kitten was on the roof by climbing up there herself. I realized that she couldn't help him get down and I was "being summoned" to lend a hand.

Rescue was easier said than done, because the pergola roof was quite high and getting down required either climbing down the rungs face first, or else jumping from the roof to a tree next to the pergola, from which it is an easy descent.

I racked my brain trying to figure out what to do. Luckily I had two teaching assistants from the university in my home at the time and one of them managed to come up with a solution. We took a broom and tied a large wicker basket to the end. We stood near the pergola and lifted the contraption to the roof. All the kitten had to do was jump about two feet into the basket. But by that time the kitten was so terrified that it was a long time before he could be convinced to make the jump. Finally he jumped and was safely lowered to the ground. Sophie was waiting for him there. She grabbed him in her mouth and ran with him toward her other kittens.

Getting kittens down from trees that were not very tall—though they undoubtedly seemed quite tall to the kitten stranded up there—was a common occurrence. So was protecting kittens from large male cats who were strangers to the community. But it was always the same mothers that didn't abandon their weak or sickly kittens and that defended their kittens when they got in trouble. Other mothers displayed complete indifference.

This brings me to a question that is worth exploring. I've tried to understand what makes some female cats devoted mothers, while others are more indifferent mothers. Apart from a small number of kittens that had a father figure in their lives, for most kittens the dominant role model—in fact, the only role model—is their mother. So the key clearly lies in the female cat's personality. But as with humans, the question arises about what primarily influences a cat's personality, nature, nurture, or a combination of the two. What factor has the greater influence?

Since I had watched future mother cats grow up, I could clearly see that daughters of devoted mothers became devoted mothers themselves, while daughters of indifferent mothers became uncaring mothers. Unfortunately, these observations are not enough to answer the question of nature or nurture, and the answer, again, seems to be some combination of the two. Kittens behaved and reacted as they were taught by their mothers, which means imitation also plays an important role.

In one area, their reaction to human touch, my observations have taught me that the dominant factor is genetics, and education plays only a secondary role. If a mother let me stroke her, her kittens would allow it too. If a mother did not consent to be touched, neither did her kittens. After they grew up and separation from the mother took place, male kittens behaved differently from females. While females continued behaving as before, most male kittens would let me stroke them and enjoyed being in physical contact with me even if their mothers kept their distance.

Many female kittens that I raised by myself from the age of one month and upward, for whom I was a mother, let me pick them up, not to mention pet them. These female kittens changed their behavior once they grew up, and they increasingly maintained their distance from me. In contrast, the male kittens that I raised continued to love attention even as adults. The marked difference in behavior of males and females shows that the critical factor here is genetics.

As I've said, I saw many interesting expressions of cooperation between females that were friends and became mothers. Before the pergola was built in the garden, when the number of cats was reasonable, I could closely follow mothers' behavior, whose principal features I've already described.

When the pergola was built and I began implementing the neutering and spaying program, the number of births in the yard decreased, as did the number of cats that brought their kittens to grow up in the cat pergola or the little yard. This is why in the last few years, I unfortunately haven't had the privilege of seeing the phenomena of motherhood that I used to see all those years ago when there were so many births in the garden.

Chapter 6:
Beauty and Colomina:
A Mother-Daughter Friendship

This chapter also relates to motherhood, but the focus is on a unique relationship between two extraordinary cats: a mother and a daughter.

Beauty arrived in my garden nine months after Kitsushi turned the garden into her home while raising her kittens. I have no idea who Beauty's mother was or from which territory she came.

As I described in the second chapter, Beauty was a white cat with black and brown patches, some of which had a leopard-like pattern. Beauty's coat was hard to describe. But it was clear that she was markedly different from the other residents of the garden. The shape of her large and beautiful head stood out, as did her tail, which throughout her life was as thin as a shoelace.

In time, once I realized that much could be learned about a cat's health by the shape of its tail, I wondered how Beauty managed to be an exception to this rule. Judging from the appearance of her tail, she should have been on her deathbed, but Beauty lived for a little more than twelve years and gave birth twice a year many kittens who survived. In fact, a significant number of the cats in my territory today are Beauty's descendants.

The garden cats accepted Beauty not with love, but with respect; bonds of friendship never formed between them. When her offspring began populating the garden alongside Kitsushi's family, a peaceful coexistence was established between the two families, but it was always clear which cat belonged to which family.

When Beauty came to me, she was already six months old. Until her first litter, she came for meals three times a day and would then disappear. She never occupied one of the cat houses nor showed an interest in doing so. After her meals, she sometimes sat for a short while on the grass and warmed herself in the sun. Afterward she would leap out of the garden and vanish. One day when I came outside, I saw Beauty slowly stroll along the path between the neighbor's homes, climb up on a log that separated our path from the neighbor's garden, and disappear.

During her first winter with us, it seemed that Beauty didn't suffer from the cold or rain more than the garden cats. I never learned exactly where Beauty lived and raised her kittens, but it was clearly a good, safe place.

The first time that Beauty got pregnant, I wondered where she would give birth. Given her attitude toward my garden, its occupants, and the cat houses, I figured that Beauty would choose to give birth where she lived rather than in the garden. That's exactly how it happened. Beauty disappeared for two days and returned thinner but without her kittens. At first she came to feed only once a day and she quickly devoured great quantities of food. Eventually she began to show up twice a day. Only after a month did she show up three times a day.

During that time, I would sometimes give the cats pieces of chicken. Beauty would eat the cat food, but once her kittens were about two months old, I noticed that she always kept at least two pieces of chicken nearby that she shielded with her body. I watched how she would pick up the two pieces in her mouth, leap out of the garden, and disappear. It was obvious that Beauty was taking the pieces of chicken to her kittens, which I still hadn't seen.

Three months after Beauty had been coming to the garden for meals three times a day, I went outside one day and there, on the landing near the door, lay four kittens with Beauty beside them. Beauty's kittens were always a colorful bunch and looked different from the other garden residents.

When I saw the whole family lying near the front entrance, I got scared. I thought Beauty had brought them to the front door so they could live under the entrance among the firewood we stored there, and in the small adjacent garden. The neighbors would not have approved of cats eating out front, to put it mildly. It was clear that if I wanted to avoid clashes with the neighbors, possibly even a tragedy, I couldn't let Beauty and her kittens remain there.

Luckily, this wasn't Beauty's intention. As I stood there watching the new family that had appeared in such an inconvenient location, Beauty ran off, disappeared, and returned with a bone. She placed the bone near the kittens. It was enough to let me know that she had brought the kittens to be fed, since they were now too big to be satisfied by mother's milk and the occasional pieces of chicken that Beauty brought them. At that point, Beauty had clearly decided not to bring the kittens into the garden with its occupants, and since she was a very smart cat, I trusted her judgment.

As described earlier, I had found a way of feeding cats in front of the house without the neighbors realizing what was happening. I would come out with a full plate of food, hide Beauty and her kittens with my body, wait for them to finish the food, take the plate out to the trash, and if the kittens made a mess, I would immediately clean up after them.

When the kittens finished eating, Beauty would emit a sound—the most motherly of sounds that I had ever heard any female make—and the kittens, like little soldiers, would surround her and the group would run up the path in front of the neighboring homes, climb up the log separating the path from a neighbor's garden, and vanish from sight. This scene took place at first once a day, then twice a day, and finally, when the kittens grew up and were about four months old, three times a day.

When spring arrived, Beauty and her kittens could be found sprawled out around the little garden near the front entrance, enjoying the sun and playing kitten games. When one of the neighbors appeared on the path, Beauty and the kittens would immediately disappear under my car, which was usually parked near the little garden.

Finally, when the kittens were four and a half months old, after about a month and a half of the acrobatics of feeding and hiding, Beauty taught them how to come to the garden. Since all her offspring were as independent and brave as she was, there weren't any problems between her kittens and the garden kittens. Beauty's kittens arrived, and in a day or two, their garden mealtimes were a done deal. The community that lived in the garden accepted and respected new arrivals.

And yet not a single kitten made my garden its home. When they grew up, the kittens occupied other gardens within my cat community's territory.

Some of Beauty's kittens contracted feline distemper or a bad cold. Beauty would bring the sick kitten to me and I would do my best to make it well again. When I treated a kitten, Beauty would watch me closely, making sure I didn't dare take him away. I couldn't always cure the kittens, and throughout the years, a significant number of Beauty's kittens passed away around the age of three or four months.

Beauty never let me touch her. When it came to avoiding human touch, Pishoosh, Sophie, and Beauty were the most extreme. The females Beauty gave birth to behaved just like her. I couldn't touch them, but they, like their mother, would rub up against me, especially against my legs, and would often purr with pleasure and affection, perhaps even love.

Beauty never left me. During the last year of her life, after two years of not giving birth, she visibly started to grow older and in the last two months it seemed that she was getting weaker too. I considered calling a cat catcher so I could bring her to the veterinarian, but I decided against it. I thought that if I were to ask Beauty what she wanted, she would clearly say that she wished to die as she had lived—independent and in nature.

I did all that I could to make her final months easier and more pleasant. I gave her the excellent food that she particularly liked, and I made sure that she was not disturbed until she finished eating.

Beauty passed away one gray autumn day after a week of looking particularly bad. I constantly followed her with my eyes to monitor her condition. That morning she still ate with the other cats, but she looked exhausted. In the afternoon, my instincts told me to go out to the yard to see if Beauty was there and check up on her. I went out to the yard but couldn't see Beauty. Again, intuition led me to the cat beds in the cat pergola, a place that Beauty never frequented, and there I saw her, lying in one of the beds. I approached her. She tried to stand up and then collapsed right in front of me. I called a friend who immediately came to my aid and together we put—or rather, he put—Beauty inside the cat bed where she lay and ran to the vet whose clinic was within walking distance. After about two hours, the young and idealistic veterinarian who worked in the clinic called to say that Beauty had arrived with hypothermia and that she and the veterinarian who owned the clinic were trying to warm her up and restore her normal body temperature. "Who knows," she said, "we might be able to cure her." I knew their attempts would fail because Beauty's day had come, but I appreciated the devotion of the new veterinarians (a man and a woman) that I discovered because of this incident.

Beauty held on for one more day. She might have survived for a short while longer, but when we found out that she had a malignant tumor at a very advanced stage, I asked the veterinarians not to torture her with further tests and to end her suffering. They agreed and Beauty was put down.

I was in mourning for a long time and only the memories of Beauty's beautiful life finally helped me overcome the sadness.

In Beauty's first litter, there was a particularly distinctive kitten with very different and interesting coloring. She was a white cat with a few ginger and black patches, and a tail that was magnificently decorated with one white stripe, one ginger stripe, and a single black stripe. I named her Colomina.

Though Beauty had given birth to numerous kittens before and after this kitten, she developed a special relationship only with Colomina. Over time, the two became close friends and joint mothers.

Colomina knew where Beauty lived since she had been born there. Of Beauty's offspring, Colomina was the only one that went to live with her mother, and Beauty seemed to welcome this. I saw how Colomina ran along the path between the houses countless times, climb across a tree log, and disappear into a nearby garden.

Colomina followed Beauty and learned everything that she could from her. Like her mother, she was highly intelligent and even outside mating season it was a pleasure to see them running together to eat and then disappearing up the path.

Colomina was certainly aware of just how beautiful and unique she was. She constantly walked around with her tail held high, and this became her trademark. Colomina wasn't a particularly large cat. Beauty was also an average-sized cat. But there was no ignoring Colomina, and passersby with their children would always stop when she walked by with her tail jutting up toward the sky.

Colomina and I formed a special, warm relationship. Though she never let me touch her, she walked beside me when I went outside and accompanied me to the road. Sometimes she waited for me outside just so we could take our little walk together. I enjoyed our strolls as much as she did. She always knew to watch out for cats and never crossed the busy road.

Colomina was a true aristocrat. She never meowed when I came out to distribute food. She never fought over food with other cats. Instead, the way she sat quietly exuding self-confidence that made the other cats make room for her near a decent plate.

Like her mother, Colomina never slept in one of the cat houses, and she only appeared in the garden during mealtimes. On rare occasions, during pleasant sunny days, she would stay for a while on the grass, but she never approached the other cats and even when she was a kitten she never played with them.

Colomina continued to thrive and when she was almost a year old, she became pregnant for the first time. Her pregnancy occurred at the same time that Beauty became pregnant. This is nature's way; almost all females get pregnant simultaneously. But when it came to Beauty and

Colomina, it almost seemed that they may have intentionally arranged it. After six weeks, they both disappeared for two days and returned on the same day, one for breakfast and the other for lunch.

During the first two weeks after giving birth, Beauty and Colomina appeared for meals once or twice a day, usually each arriving alone. They ate quickly and then ran away and vanished. After two weeks, Colomina appeared for breakfast by herself, took her time eating, and even stayed for half an hour to enjoy the sun. She looked at the kittens that had been born in the garden and kept her distance from the mothers. At noon Beauty appeared alone, ate leisurely, sat on one of the wicker couches, and took a quick nap. For the last meal of the day, both of them appeared together and, again, they ate quickly and then disappeared.

This pattern repeated itself daily in different variations for several weeks. By now, it's probably obvious to readers what was happening—Beauty and Colomina were raising their kittens together, babysitting each other's kittens to allow each other to take longer breaks.

I was extremely curious to see Colomina's kittens. I tried my luck and crawled over the log into the neighboring garden. I didn't see a thing. I started walking from garden to garden, focusing on the areas at the back, but I could not find Beauty, Colomina, or their kittens. I called out their names in vain. The tantalizing food I was carrying also didn't help. Not a sound could be heard from anywhere. After about an hour and a half I gave up and returned home. As with Beauty, so it was with Colomina, and until her last day, I never knew where she gave birth.

I calculated when the kittens should be old enough to eat something by themselves, and when the two females appeared together for a meal, I put pieces of chicken near them so they could take them to their kittens. I imagined that Beauty would teach Colomina how to carry several pieces of chicken in her mouth—and so she did. Both females ran out of the garden with pieces of chicken in their mouths, on their way back to their kittens.

Naturally I wondered when he two matrons would appear at my front door, and if Colomina would bring her kittens to the front of the house as well. The thought of eight or even twelve kittens sprawled across the doormat at the entrance and the neighbors' response really scared me, for hiding eight to twelve kittens would be a daunting task.

It seemed that Beauty may have understood the problem that would arise if all the kittens arrived together, and so the first day only four kittens appeared at the front entrance. Beauty accompanied them and I was certain that these were her kittens. Two of them had coats similar to Beauty's, but one was a calico and another was black and white.

Though Beauty's previous kittens were different colors, there had never been a black and white kitten before and the calico looked different. I thought that she must live around males that I hadn't seen before, and they were responsible for these colors.

As in the past, I fed the kittens and managed to hide all traces of the "crime" from the neighbors. I returned home and after half an hour heard a soft meowing at the door. I opened the door and there was Beauty again, albeit with a different set of four kittens. This time the kittens looked very much like kittens Beauty had given birth to in the past.

I then understood that this second group was Beauty's own kittens, whereas earlier she had brought Colomina's kittens. I went to prepare a plate of food and the clandestine meal was repeated. As I shielded the group with my body so the neighbors walking along the path would not be able to see what was happening, I turned my head and saw Colomina with her four kittens at the end of the path.

The next morning Beauty appeared with her kittens and Colomina. There was no trace of Colomina's kittens. I looked down the path and there, sitting on the tree log for all to see, was a group of kittens. I couldn't quite make them out at that distance.

When Beauty's kittens had had their fill, the two mothers and the kittens leaped down the path toward the log. I stood there watching and after a few minutes, Colomina came running back, followed by her four offspring. I moved a little to make room for them on the landing. Colomina proudly showed off her kittens and I did as she expected and provided food.

This far from simple operation lasted for about a month, and since Beauty and Colomina each gave birth about twenty times, I went through this ordeal often. A neighbor caught me only once, and he was surprisingly forgiving about the whole affair, perhaps because I made sure to clean up after every meal—and perhaps the sight of these magnificent families melted his heart a little. Who knows?

Let's return to Colomina's first litter. Having learned from Beauty to bring her kittens to the front entrance, she also learned to bring me any sick or weak kittens. As I said, taking care of Beauty's kittens caused me much grief because I couldn't always save them. But while Beauty guarded her kittens like a lioness to making sure I only gave them their medicine and didn't pick them up while under her watchful eye, Colomina allowed me to carry a sick kitten in my hands from time to time. However, she never let me touch the healthy kittens, so there was no possibility of vaccinating them at an early age. But Colomina's sick kittens did receive treatment at the vet's office. Unfortunately, the veterinarian also had only limited success.

Colomina learned all the motherly arts from Beauty, and her kittens were as well-groomed, courageous, and independent as Beauty's.

But it was clear that the reverse was also happening and that Beauty was learning from her daughter. Colomina had a particular method of carrying kittens in her mouth and Beauty began to imitate her. Colomina also discovered that it was possible to teach kittens to jump off the log between the path and the garden when they were even younger. Colomina allowed me to accompany her and her kittens—or Beauty's kittens, if they were with her—several times to the log. I saw how Colomina ordered the kittens to gather at the end of the log, which faced the neighboring garden, and repeatedly showed them how she jumped from the edge of the log into the garden. Sometimes she would grab a kitten in her mouth, though they weren't small any longer, and jumped with it. And so I learned how Colomina moved her kittens before they learned how to jump by themselves. Sometimes after she jumped she would emit a special sound, which probably meant, "Now it's your turn." At least one of the kittens would muster the courage to jump. After one kitten made the jump, the others were less fearful and they gathered their courage and jumped as well. Sometimes after she showed them how to jump back up onto the log, Colomina would gently push one of her kittens until he had no choice but to jump.

One time I saw Beauty standing and watching these jumping exercises, and on one rare occasion I saw Beauty act just like Colomina.

One might ask how I can be so certain that Beauty learned this behavior from Colomina and not the other way around. This is a valid question. The answer has more to do with intuition that knowledge. My intuition was based on the fact that Colomina was a better jumper than her mother, though neither cat was a particularly strong jumper or climber.

When their kittens grew up, both Beauty and Colomina left them completely without supervision for longer periods each day. The final act of leaving their kittens occurred simultaneously for both cats.

The two ate in the garden. Colomina learned from Beauty when to bring kittens to the garden and to stop eating bringing them to the front entrance. Little by little they began ignoring the kittens' plates. By that point the kittens had learned to eat with other cats. Finally the two females completely severed ties with their kittens that were nearly five months old by then, and the two females would drive them away if they approached in search of a motherly hug.

When it came to affairs of the heart, both cats were shy and I never saw them in the act of mating. They conducted their lovemaking in other gardens.

When Beauty stopped giving birth, she devoted all her time to helping Colomina give birth and raise her kittens. Nothing was as touching or as sad as watching Beauty assist Colomina in rearing her offspring when Beauty was unable to have more of her own.

When Beauty's health declined, Colomina, who was a year younger than her mother, also fell ill. She passed away just six months after her mother died.

As with Beauty, so with Colomina, and I decided against calling the noose-wielding cat catcher, which meant that I didn't bring her to the veterinarian. I was sure that she would have preferred to live her final days as an independent cat in her natural surroundings. I pampered her as well during the final weeks of her life. Like Beauty, she came to the yard to live out her final days there. Beauty came to me during her final hours, while Colomina came in her last days. The moment I saw Colomina lying on a piece of cardboard in the yard I realized her condition was serious. When she let me touch her and stroke her, I could feel that she was skin and bones. Despite her great courage—like Beauty, she still ate lunch—I saw that she was suffering. I decided to spare her a few days of pain and she let me put her in a cage without resisting. I think she almost welcomed it. She simply trusted me after our many years together. We brought her to the veterinarian who took one look at her and saw that she had no hope of surviving. He didn't even offer to perform tests or try to cure her. He thought she had only a few days of intense suffering left. With a heavy heart and with love I said goodbye to her at the veterinarian's clinic, where she was put to sleep. I saw it as an act of kindness.

Anyone who has raised animals at home or in a garden knows the heartache that is involved. The lifespan of a dog or a cat is significantly shorter than that of a person, and it is part of the natural course of things that we bury the animals we've raised. Sometimes pet owners immediately adopt another dog or cat. I had no need to do that. One cat passed away and twenty more remained. However, the presence of other cats could not make up for the loss of any particular cat.

Those who care for many animals, like me and others who take care of street cats, find that grief is an almost constant companion in the face of disease, our limited ability to help in many cases, and the inevitable death of cats at a relatively young age, given that the lifespan of a street cat is at most twelve years.

I believe that Beauty and Colomina lived full lives as street cats that had a caretaker to provide food and other necessities. They also knew how to enjoy every single aspect of their lives. In other words, they had highly developed life skills. They went through all the experiences that a female street cat can undergo. They established friendships, raised kittens with love and devotion, enjoyed their mating seasons, and loved being pregnant and giving birth. They also found themselves a home, the location of which remains a mystery to this day.

From what I could gather, they clearly understood the dangers of the street: cars and other vehicles, cat haters, dogs that were dangerous to cats, violent cats, well-intentioned but harmful children, and more. They managed to avoid all these dangers for twelve years and actually died from diseases related to old age.

Even as adults, they never stopped playing interesting games with their kittens or with each other. Beauty always seemed busy, and when one encountered her on the street, she appeared to be in a hurry, intent on some task. Colomina was an inspiration with her sense of the good life. When I met her on the street, she seemed to be on her way to some party, concert, or play.

I never saw one of them feeling bored. The number of litters they had filled their lives, as they were both deadly serious about their role as mothers. But even when they were between litters, they always found something to do. Colomina loved lying in the sun for long periods of time. Beauty tended to play in the sun for shorter lengths of time. She mostly liked to go to the big empty lot, overgrown with wild flowers and bushes, located behind some nearby houses. She would remain there among the flowers, though she always seemed to choose a different flower each time. How did I know this? At first flowers tended to get stuck in her fur, and every so often I would see her decorated with different flowers. Also, the few times that I went to the big lot in search of a cat that had vanished and might have been ill, I saw Beauty among the bushes and flowers, and each time she was in a different spot.

Since I also specialize in the subject of happiness and wrote the book *The Mirage of Happiness*, I must say that, in principle, I think that happiness is not the goal of life. It cannot be the goal of life, nor should it be. I also think it is not possible to learn to be happy.

I agree that there are two definitions of happiness. The first defines happiness as an overall satisfaction with life as a whole. This is a cognitive definition. One contemplates one's life as a whole and decides where to place it on a scale of happiness from zero to ten. The second definition consists of peaks of all-consuming happiness, in which the sky seems bluer, the grass greener, and one loves the entire world, wanting for nothing. This is a more emotive definition and here one can only testify to having experienced such peaks, which by their nature are short-lived, given our innate tendency to adapt to every situation.

I reflect on happiness here because I want to say that Beauty and Colomina were happy cats according to both definitions. Regarding the emotive definition, it was clear that they experienced peaks of happiness numerous times, especially when they were in each other's company or in the company of their young kittens. The joy they often exhibited was marvelous.

As for the cognitive definition, one could argue that a cat cannot contemplate its life as a whole, that its perception of time differs from ours, and so on. These are all valid arguments. However, as someone who observed Beauty and Colomina for years, I can swear that sometimes I saw them sitting perfectly calm and peaceful with a look on their faces that in my opinion expressed their feeling that their life as a whole was going just splendidly. They were happy cats because their life skills enabled them to live their lives to the fullest and enjoy what the world around them had to offer. Their curiosity, patience, and devotion helped make their lives happy. And when hard times came, they knew how to accept them stoically, always keeping a sense of perspective.

Did Beauty pass on her capacity for happiness to Colomina? There is no doubt that she passed on the right genes. Did the way she raised Colomina contribute to her daughter's ability to be happy? I think Beauty's kitten-rearing methods certainly helped Colomina by providing her with a variety of life skills.

Did Beauty's and Colomina's offspring have the same traits? I find it a difficult question to answer because each female gave birth to so many kittens that it was impossible to properly get to know every single one. But those who established a stronger relationship with me during their time in the yard—for example, cats that approached me while emitting a special sound, females that brought over their kittens to show them to me, or males that came for a monthly visit and were visibly happy to see me—these cats usually had their mothers' nature. They were confident, curious, independent, and calm.

Kitsushi's offspring, on the other hand, were more aggressive, less calm, and had a tendency to take risks. They always seemed to me to be more restless and, therefore, less happy.

Chapter 7: The One and Only Nonny

I loved and still love all the cats mentioned in this book, as well as others that are not mentioned, though I had closer relationships with the cats whose stories I've told here. But Nonny was my one and only true feline love. My relationship with him was the most beautiful relationship of my life.

Nonny appeared in my garden a year and a half after Kitsushi's and Beauty's families settled down here. Either his mother abandoned him or she was run over by a car. Another possibility is that he simply got lost. In any case, one morning I went out into the garden and saw a very small cat that was about three weeks old. He could already see, but it was clear that he had just been weaned. Nonny was a tabby, but the stripes on his coat weren't black and gray. Instead they were brownish ginger mixed with black, and his coat included a small patch of white, as did his feet.

The moment he saw me, he ran toward me in the funny way very young kittens move. I bent over and he happily let me pick him up. There was no doubt that this was love at first sight. The moment I held Nonny in my arms, I knew instantly that this kitten and I would develop a very special relationship indeed. I'm not saying this in hindsight—it really was how I felt.

I wondered whether I should take him home and raise him as a house cat or leave him outside and raise him in the garden. I decided to let the kitten choose for himself. I brought Nonny into the living room and left the door to the garden open. Nonny ran around the living room and after a few minutes gleefully ran out into the garden. He decided to grow up outdoors. Since at that time most of the other occupants of the garden were Kitsushi's offspring and a few belonged to Beauty, I didn't know how Nonny would be received. But it turned out that they liked this special kitten, and after I prepared a place for him to sleep (it was summer then), no cat tried to take over his spot.

Nonny

In the part of the garden next to the living room there was a small square paved with Jerusalem stones, and that's where the cat houses and sleeping spots were located. In summer, sleeping arrangements consisted of either cardboard boxes padded with newspapers and old clothes, or open plastic beds, again padded with newspapers and rags. Once more I let Nonny choose. I prepared two kinds of beds and without hesitation he jumped into the cardboard one.

Now I had to prepare food for Nonny. All the other kittens were still nursing and would only occasionally take a bite of the adults' food. Nonny, on the other hand, needed to receive all his nourishment from me.

Equipped with baby formula and soft kitten food, I went out into the garden and walked over to Nonny, who was lying in his bed and looking around with immense curiosity. All the other cats seemed to have adjusted to the new stranger and weren't paying him any special attention. I knelt down near Nonny and set a bowl of baby formula next to him. To my delight, he drank a bit, paused as if deciding whether this strange stuff was any good, determined that it was, and continued drinking with vigor. His reaction to the kitten food was also positive, if not extremely so, and he ate some of what I had prepared for him with gusto. It seemed that the capacity of his stomach was smaller than I had estimated. In this way, I continued to raise Nonny, who during this time let me pet him, pick him up, and play with him.

Sometimes, when he showed signs of wanting to enter the living room, I would bring him inside. With time he discovered the armchair in the corner of the basement and made it his bed, even though I also provided him with a soft and comfortable cat bed.

In the garden, meanwhile, Nonny was becoming a hit. The other kittens, which were more or less his age, sought him out and included him in their games. Nonny willingly complied, and once he grasped the essence of the kittens' games, he began initiating new ones.

The moment he would leave his bed or the house, kittens would run toward him and Nonny would organize—yes, actually organize—a group game. Sometime it would be an attack game, with Nonny dividing the kittens into two teams that would fight each other, in jest or in earnest, with the kittens jumping on one another, knocking one another down, biting (quite gently, I believe), and so on. At a certain point Nonny would stop playing, and soon afterward the rest of the kittens would also end the game. During these months, I could never figure out who had won, or if anyone was even keeping track.

Though I observed Nonny's games at length, I was mainly interested in seeing that each time he invented new additions to the games, he would teach the other kittens what they had to do. I was especially intrigued by the speed at which the kittens learned, and how they would play each game quite deliberately.

Ever since the first litter in my garden—remember, this was Kitsushi's litter and where our story began—it was clear to me that the games kittens played had educational value; they provided them with life skills and prepared them to enter the world of adults.

Interestingly, from an early age males and females played the same games and I couldn't discern a preference for particular games based on gender. It seemed that during the first two months of playing these games, skills were learned that would be needed by both genders in the future. Both males and females had to learn how to hold their ground, occasionally fight for a better sleeping spot or for food, drive away enemies of various kinds, and acquire allies. In short, these were games that taught various forms of cooperation, offense, and defense.

Only at a later stage, when kittens reached six months of age, could male kittens be seen from time to time playing games of wrestling and attack among themselves; female kittens generally didn't participate. Females preferred games that were more fun, like jumping and leaping in strange ways on a bug that crossed their path, or playing with their and other kittens' tails. They clearly focused on games that would better prepare them for the time when they would need to amuse their own kittens during the early days when kittens play with their mother.

However, the most interesting thing of all was to see how Nonny gradually became the undisputed leader of the kittens. This occurred despite the fact that Nonny was not a particularly large kitten and there were other, bigger male kittens in the garden.

From my observations, I determined that the kittens complied with Nonny's wishes for three main reasons. First, Nonny had something to offer the kittens. He always came up with interesting ideas for new games. Unlike him, the other kittens tended to play the same games over and over again. Second, Nonny exuded a sense of confidence and power, which he mainly expressed in his calm and quiet manner. Other kittens often exhibited insecurity, which manifested itself when kittens hid under a bush or prematurely ran away from a game they found too aggressive. Other cats did not exhibit the same calm that Nonny had. Instead, they were anxious and impatient. During mealtimes, Nonny never ran up to the plates but rather quietly made his way toward one of them. In contrast, quite a few kittens did immediately run toward a plate and some of them moved between plates with marked disquiet. Third, Nonny was very stubborn and he stood his ground not only for himself, but also for other kittens that seemed to need protection. During mealtimes, for instance, if Nonny noticed that a kitten was left standing near a plate without access to the food—the result not necessarily of malice, but rather of a feeding frenzy—he would approach the kitten, stand next to it, and, to my utter amazement, push it near a plate. As if by magic, the feeding cats would immediately make room for Nonny and he would push the rescued kitten into the newly created space and wait until he saw him eat. Only then did he return to his own plate, or begin eating from the same plate as the kitten.

In time, the kittens learned that Nonny helped the weak and they began to signal him with special sounds when in distress. In most cases

Nonny would appear. Sometimes he didn't hear the kittens or thought they weren't really in need, or else he figured that the kitten had to learn how to deal with the problem by itself, in which case he would observe the meowing kitten and stay where he was.

Nonny grew up and reached sexual maturity. At that time, Geezer was the leader of my community of street cats, and he took particular care to drive away almost all males that reached adulthood except a few that didn't challenge his leadership and were content with their role in his "warm-up act."

When it came to Nonny, things were different. There was no doubt that Nonny would not have been content as assistant to the leader, but would have sought leadership for himself. Even though Nonny did not hide his intentions, Geezer developed a special attitude toward him. It seemed that he wanted to prepare him to be his successor. It's not clear to me how they came to this understanding, but the reality of life in the garden made it obvious that Nonny was Geezer's protégé. He accompanied Geezer during mating season, and I saw him learn the art of courtship and mating and the way that Geezer would allocate different roles to the males that formed his "warm-up act." As I've already mentioned, the purpose of the "warm-up act" was to vigorously court a female and wear her down so that Geezer would be left with the relatively easy task of a short courtship and first mating. Afterward, Geezer would let the members of the "warm-up act" mate with the female, and they would fight among themselves for the privilege of being the second-in-command.

Nonny never joined the "warm-up act" in wearing down a female, but he remained close to Geezer. After Geezer won over the cat, Nonny was given the right to court her and mate with her. Only afterward would members of the "warm-up act" get their chance.

Geezer was a faithful husband to Kitsushi. It seemed, therefore, that mating with other females didn't hold much meaning for him, and as far as I could tell, he gladly passed the females on to Nonny.

Since Geezer helped Kitsushi look after the kittens as they grew up, and then he would disappear from the garden with Kitsushi once she decided that her maternal role had come to an end for that litter, there were times when Geezer did not function as a leader. Little by little, Nonny began taking over the role during these times, and the cats got used to having two leaders. During mating season and kitten rearing, Geezer was the leader, but the rest of the time it was Nonny.

As I've already mentioned, in time Nonny became the uncontested leader of my community. As we will see in the chapter on leadership, however, his reign was not a long one and lasted for only two years.

After a cat named Stripy took over as leader, which is a story that has already been told and will be further developed later, Nonny became the leader of a small but devoted group of living near the front entrance of the house. Nonny was not satisfied with his role and when he was four years old, he began going on increasingly longer walks. He would disappear for a week or ten days and return tired and hungry, tap on the front door, go downstairs to his bed, and sleep like the dead. Only after he woke up would he bother to eat.

After every prolonged period of absence, events would repeat themselves, and so my house became the place where Nonny recuperated. Because of his numerous absences, however, he stopped being a part of the community. The group of his followers at the front of the house slowly broke up as Nonny's excursions grew longer and longer. In time, the group reunited with Stripy's group. Nonny must have completely given up his membership in my community and instead chose a life of wandering punctuated by rest and recuperation at my home.

One night after Nonny had been gone for longer than ten days, I heard a knock at the door. I was already asleep but I had grown accustomed to responding to any taps at the door. I got up, opened the door, and there was Nonny. At first all I could see was how exhausted and thin he looked. But a few moments after he began his descent into the basement, and as I followed him, I saw that his tail was in an odd position. I didn't understand what had happened and thought that Nonny was dragging his tail from fatigue. But when we got to the basement and Nonny approached the water bowl that was always there for him, I went over to pet him. When I touched his back, near his tail, he recoiled in pain. I immediately realized that something had happened to Nonny's tail and perhaps his back. Very gently I touched his tail and he didn't respond. It almost seemed like his tail was paralyzed.

I became increasingly anxious that Nonny had a serious spinal injury and that his tail was paralyzed or broken. Despite how late it was, I called one of the veterinarians who took care of my cats, and she agreed to see Nonny immediately.

I gently picked Nonny up and put him in the cage that I always kept there in the basement, as if it stood there waiting for trouble to happen. The cage was lined with a little blanket and several newspapers. I took Nonny and we drove to Mevaseret Zion, a suburb of Jerusalem, where the clinic was located. When we got to the clinic, I carefully took the cage out of the car, wanting to avoid any unnecessary movement that might hurt Nonny.

The veterinarian examined him and asked me to leave him overnight for further tests to be performed the following day. I knew that the quality of care in this little clinic was very good, so with a heavy heart I said goodbye to Nonny, who by that time was almost sound asleep due to his extreme exhaustion. I returned home. The next day I waited for the moment the clinic opened for business and called to find out how Nonny was doing. I was told that he was much better after a good night's rest and that his appetite was normal. I was asked to come in the afternoon, after they completed their tests, and then I could hear an update on Nonny's condition.

That afternoon I dutifully arrived at the clinic and the vet explained that Nonny's tail was broken in two places, but that there was no damage to his spinal cord. In addition, Nonny was malnourished and generally quite weak. I was told that all that Nonny needed was proper rest and food and that his tail would mend on its own with time.

I happily returned home with Nonny. The entire basement was ready for him. Assuming that he might find it difficult at first to jump onto his favorite armchair, I added an extra blanket to the already comfortable cat bed that was always on the floor. And of course I put a plate heaped with his favorite food next to a bowl of water.

Nonny's recuperation lasted three weeks. His overall health improved, but while his tail could be moved, it would never again be held high. I knew that as long as Nonny didn't ask to go outside, his recuperation wasn't yet at an end, and it was clear to me that the moment he felt like himself again he would demand to leave. In the meantime, I enjoyed Nonny's constant companionship; he had never before stayed indoors for so long.

I had hoped that Nonny would grow used to life inside and would become a house cat with the occasional brief excursion outdoors. But my hopes were dashed. At the end of his third week indoors, Nonny began showing signs that he wanted to go outside. When he came upstairs with his tail slightly raised and tapped on the door, I had no choice but to open it.

His first walk was very brief and within an hour I heard a knock at the door. Nonny was waiting for me, and he returned indoors, visibly satisfied. From that day on, he began sleeping less and less and spent most of his time strolling around the house and making short excursions outside. It seemed that these outdoor walks increased his confidence and restored his longing for the life he had led in nature. In any case, at the end of the fourth week Nonny seemed ready for a long walk. When he asked to go out I had a feeling—my intuition was quite strong when it came to Nonny—that this time he wouldn't return after a few hours or even a few days. I felt that this time he would be absent for a much longer period of time.

Nonny did in fact resume his normal walks, which progressively became longer and longer. This continued for six months. Nonny's tail never went back to normal, and I was afraid that this would be an obstacle when jumping and maneuvering through difficult places, as a cat's tail is not merely ornamental but also navigational. Nevertheless, Nonny must have adapted to his new condition and continued his life as before.

One winter evening I heard a tap at the door and found Nonny waiting for me, soaked to the bone. I took one look at him and knew that he wasn't doing very well, to put it mildly. Nonny looked as if he had suddenly aged, when in fact he was still a relatively young cat. It was as if he had lost his spirit. He slowly went down to his armchair and quickly fell asleep. Over the next few days he never left that armchair except to eat and drink a little and use the litter box.

I concluded that Nonny was suffering from depression or some chronic disease. I decided to take him to the veterinarian, and the same woman who had taken care of his tail saw us. She took a blood sample, examined him, and confirmed what I already knew: he was not himself. We had to wait for the test results to see if he was ill, but it was clear that he wasn't doing well. When the results of the blood tests came back, the veterinarian called to let me know that everything looked normal. However, she agreed that Nonny was going through a difficult time.

I tried everything I could think of to cheer him up, from cajoling him to play to enticing him with food. I also spent a lot of time keeping him company, talking to him, and petting him. Each time he gave me a loving but wretched look. I still hoped that time would heal whatever it was that troubled Nonny and that his usual vitality would return. But nothing changed. After a couple of days Nonny did start going out on short walks for an hour or two, but the walks didn't seem to do him any good. I never found out what had happened to Nonny, but for some reason he lost his interest in life. He was a cat suffering from depression.

In my grief, I started reading more books about cats, talked to friends who had cats, and spoke again to the veterinarian who had cared for him. They all gave me the same advice and in fact suggested that I do exactly what I was already doing: give Nonny lots of love and affection.

Days passed and then weeks, and Nonny's condition didn't improve. Suddenly, one morning as soon as I got up I saw Nonny sitting near the front door, anxiously waiting for me to open it. I thought I could see in his eyes a glimmer of the old and healthy Nonny. I let him out with mixed feelings and a heavy heart. Nonny went outside and I followed him to see where he was going. As he reached the end of the path that led to the road, he turned his head and stared at me for a long time. That was the last look that Nonny ever gave me. He went away and never returned.

Almost eight years have passed since Nonny left, and not a day goes by that I don't think of him. No other cat ever took Nonny's place in my heart, and no cat ever will. Sometimes, when I sit in the living room in my favorite armchair, I can actually see Nonny looking at me with his usual look, his eyes halfway closed.

There is no doubt in my mind that Nonny was an exceptional cat. Any attempt to compare him to a dog would fail. Nonny had all the characteristics of a cat, but he was a "human" cat. With him, communication was a two-way street. His understanding exceeded that of any cat I have ever known. And the love that he felt for me and the ways in which he expressed it were uniquely his. He was a street cat, but he let me care for him as if he were a perfectly domesticated house cat. He was always considerate and during the times he stayed in the house he never bothered me. He would wait until I finished what I was doing, and then he would ask to go out or play. Even during his illness and depression, Nonny never complained, and I never heard a single whimper of distress pass his lips. His eyes said it all.

Though Nonny could be cruel toward other males that, as a leader, he wanted to chase out of his territory, Nonny was always gentle and tender with me.

What does my heart tell me about Nonny's fate? I have no doubt that he embarked on his last walk, knowing perfectly well that this would be the final journey of his life. How he died, I do not know, but I am sure he passed away soon after he left the house that last time.

Not a day, sometimes not an hour, goes by that I don't thank God for giving me a few years of the kind of love and friendship that I had with Nonny. During hard times, I think of Nonny and the love that existed between us and somehow things don't seem so bad. For that is the power of true love: it gives the person who experiences it the strength to deal with hardships for the rest of his or her life.

As readers know by now, I loved and continue to love a significant number of cats, some from the very bottom of my heart. Yet the kind of reciprocal love that Nonny and I shared I have yet to experience again.

Even when I compare my relationship with Nonny to the relationships I've had with the dogs that I raised (if such a comparison is even possible), I find that my relationship with Nonny was the healthiest and most mature of all. I gave Nonny complete freedom to choose how to live his life and I respected his wishes. Despite my tendency to worry too much about things, for some reason when it came to Nonny I always calmly let him go. I trusted him. Yes, I had complete confidence in Nonny. Perhaps this is why Nonny completely trusted me. Only rarely does a street cat consent to being put into a cage, or even to having someone pick it up, and Nonny was a street cat through and through. Nonny let me to do all this without a fuss. It seems to me that I could probably have driven Nonny to the veterinarian without a cage, and he would have quietly sat in the backseat.

His conduct at various veterinary clinics throughout the years was also exemplary. There was never any need to hold him down. If I stood next to him, that was enough. With all other cats, getting them inside a cage and bringing them to the veterinarian was an ordeal. Usually a cat's condition would have to be serious and the cat near exhaustion for it to be possible to put it inside a cage and for the veterinarian to treat the cat without me or someone else holding it down.

There was mutual respect between Nonny and me—we each respected the other's differences. Nonny respected the fact that I belonged to what he may have called "the bipeds," living in houses, eating at a table, and expressing emotions by relying heavily on language. I respected Nonny as a cat that, his tender heart notwithstanding, could viciously attack a competing male. There was also empathy between us. I could usually feel what Nonny felt and I have no doubt that Nonny learned to discern my emotions and mental states as well.

In my book *The Mirage of Happiness* I wrote of the need to study what we call life skills and learn how they can be taught. I argue that teaching life skills is the most important thing we can do as people living in the twenty-first century, since we must deal with a world that is both full of opportunities and highly competitive. And we must do this more or less alone.

I continue the line of thought that characterizes a significant part of the work of Erich Fromm, who identified and deeply analyzed man's fear of freedom and separateness. In his book *The Art of Love*, Fromm suggests one way of dealing with the source of all anxiety: separateness. His solution is love.

Fromm argues that learning the art of love enables a person to escape his or her separateness. I would add that, in accordance with his theory, learning how to love is also what makes it possible for us to face our fear of freedom and of the responsibility that follows. When we learn to love ourselves, we can love others. Love, according to Fromm, is characterized by concern, responsibility, respect for differences, and empathy. He sees relationships of dominance and dependency as the opposite of love.

When I read what I wrote about the special relationship I had with Nonny, I realize that in my love for Nonny there existed, perhaps for the first time in my life, the conditions of love as described by Fromm. My relationship with Nonny lacked any element of dependency or control. Although I might seem indifferent and disinterested due to my absence of anxiety that something horrible might happen to Nonny if I let him go his own way, this is a mistake. In fact the exact opposite is true. My absence of anxiety stemmed from a feeling the likes of which I had never known before. It was grounded in a deep conviction that Nonny had every right to determine the course of his life. If my love for Nonny was true, I had to give him complete freedom. My interference was justified only when Nonny needed me on at times when he couldn't take care of himself. Even in these cases, my involvement had to respect

Nonny's wishes. Without realizing it, right from the beginning of our relationship, when I let Nonny choose whether to live inside or outside, I had laid the foundation for true love. And our relationship continued to be this way. Though Nonny was partly a house cat, he stayed in my home only when he chose to do so, just as he chose the length of his recuperation. I never tried to control Nonny or make him dependent on me. Instead of a relationship of dependency and control, our relationship evolved into one of mutual trust and the acceptance that Nonny had his own life.

By nature, I am an anxious person. I am particularly anxious about those I love. This characteristic overshadowed my relationship with the dogs I raised. I never let them go for a walk without holding onto the leash. To a certain extent, this is also my relationship with other cats, such as the pergola cats that are the closest thing to house cats. An example of this is my relationship with Turqi, also known as Tushi (her original name is Turquoise), who will appear in a later chapter.

It is true that my relationship with Beauty and Colomina, cats that never entered my home, can serve as an example of a healthy relationship without any dominance or dependency. But this is hardly an accomplishment to be proud of, as it was clear from the start that they were living their lives as street cats. With respect to all the garden cats and later the yard cats, my role was clear: to assist them by providing food, shelter, medicine, and sometimes help treating their kittens. The cats' independence was absolute. But it's interesting that even in these cases I never stopped being anxious for the cats, and every morning I would check to see which of my cats were there and which looked healthy. If a particular cat went missing more than once, I was consumed by a sense of disquiet, and the same happened if I saw signs of illness.

With Nonny, as I said, I had a different relationship. It seemed to me that with Nonny I was a person who didn't suffer from anxiety.

How this came about, how I managed to develop such a healthy relationship with Nonny, I have no idea. Since I am who I am, there must have been something special about Nonny and his attitude toward me that nurtured the healthier elements in my psyche and subdued the anxious ones. Nonny always made me feel peaceful. Even when I worried about him, as I did in the beginning when he started going out on long excursions, it was a healthy kind of worrying. It didn't disturb my sleep. Deep inside I not only trusted Nonny and our relationship, but I also fully internalized—not just rationally, but emotionally and instinctively—the fact that Nonny was the master of his own fate.

Much is written today about the therapeutic value of adopting and caring for pets. What is usually meant by this is that a pet provides love and the companionship of another living creature at home. The possibility of petting the animal, playing with it, and feeding it goes a long way toward alleviating a person's loneliness and inducing calm.

In my case, all the care that I have lavished on the animals that I've had and on those that I still care for today has rarely ever induced calm or alleviated loneliness. On the contrary, many times my peace of mind and routine are disrupted by my worry for some cat. Even when I am fully absorbed in some endeavor, thoughts about a particular cat will rise to the surface—will he come back or not, and is he dead, or did he simply go somewhere else?

A recent tale of such a worry was a little tabby with a reddish coat. Her story appears in another chapter. To put it briefly, she was born in my yard as part of a highly unsuccessful litter and managed to survive. Recently she failed to appear for breakfast for the first time in her life. She had been born in the yard, had given birth in the yard, and had raised her kittens in the yard—she hardly ever left. Then suddenly she was gone. She hasn't appeared since.

Ever since this red cat disappeared, I've found myself feeling uneasy. When I think about the causes for this unease, I quickly conclude that I am concerned for the red one. If this is how I feel about this cat, readers can understand how concerned I am about the cats that I've been feeding and taking care of for years. Readers can also understand how extraordinary my relationship with Nonny was.

No wonder, then, that for me, Nonny is the one and only.

Chapter 8: Furry and Bambi, and a Little about Some Other Furries and Bambies

Furry and Bambi were born on the third anniversary of the great cat invasion. Their mother was Big Mama, so they belonged to Kitsushi's extended family.

Furry was a tabby, but long-haired and quite handsome. His brother, Bambi, was gray all over with white feet, and he was also a pleasure to behold.

Ever since I named these two cats, I have called all long-haired cats Furry, and I've used the name Bambi for all gray cats with white feet. I also add a nickname to distinguish between Furries and Bambies.

The two brothers were frequent visitors in my home and arrived via the front entrance. Furry also made it a habit to sit on the windowsill in the kitchen and from there he observed the goings-on in the house.

When they were kittens there were no problems; they ate and slept in the garden as usual. During those first seven or eight months, their lives were full of games and joy. Furry was the smarter of the two and always managed to win the sophisticated games Nonny invented, while Bambi wasn't so interested in competition and was much more curious about nature. He would approach every plant and carefully scrutinize it, smell it, and try to taste it. He would play with a branch or a leaf that fell off some plant, and he was delighted whenever a flower dropped to the ground. Bambi often jumped around the garden, chasing a flower, and sometimes I could see him with a flower briefly held in his mouth.

Even when they came indoors, the two brothers behaved nothing alike. Furry immediately jumped on me and waited to be patted and pampered, while Bambi walked around the house, went upstairs, and examined all the rooms and their contents.

Furry

It's interesting that none of the cats that came inside tried to sleep on one of the beds or armchairs upstairs, and they all found their place either on the main floor (where the living room and kitchen were located) or in the basement.

It's possible that they liked the basement because it smelled like cats. Ever since Shushka's time, and later Nonny's, there was always a cat bed and a fragrant litter box in the basement. The brothers liked the first floor because that's where I stayed most of the time; not to mention the kitchen and all its smells was also located there.

In any case, each time both cats entered the house together, Furry would run straight toward me while Bambi would quickly explore the house. The two brothers' visits were usually brief because when Bambi concluded his exploration, which was never very long, he wanted to go back out into the garden and Furry accompanied him. When they came in together, Furry must have seen it as his duty to accompany his brother outside, because when he came in the house alone—something Bambi never did—he sometimes stayed for several hours.

During Bambi's longer visits, Nonny often entered the house and went down to his armchair in the basement. Nonny would briefly glance at Furry and continue on his way, while Furry would twitch his tail because Nonny was his leader. They were not friends, but there wasn't any hostility between them. Bambi ran into Nonny only rarely, and when the two did meet, Bambi would make way for Nonny with the respect due to a leader.

When the brothers grew up and became adults at the age of eight months old, the dynamic changed dramatically.

In the yard, Furry and Bambi behaved toward Nonny as typical young males did toward their leader, and their first mating season together passed without incident. The brothers were happy to be part of Nonny's "warm-up act" and were allowed to mate several times, or at least I assume they were.

However, inside the house things were changing. After mating season was over, Nonny frequented the house quite often and so did Furry and Bambi. At first Nonny just looked at them threateningly, growling ominously, but there wasn't any physical contact between the cats. Nonny continued on his way to his armchair in the basement, and Furry remained lying on one of the sofas or armchairs in the living room. Bambi tried to get out of Nonny's way and he usually immediately disappeared upstairs somewhere. Nevertheless, the atmosphere had changed. It was no longer laid-back, and there was tension in the air.

The blowup occurred without any warning.

Nonny was just entering the house through the front door as usual, and Bambi was on his way out. In an instant Nonny lunged at Bambi and viciously attacked him. Bambi was terrified due to his complete lack of experience as the victim of violence. Most of the fighting between cats took place during mating season and involved Geezer and Nonny on one side and strange cats looking to try their luck in love on the other side. Geezer and Nonny always defeated them. Bambi was so scared that he urinated inside the house, near the door, and when Nonny released him for a second, he fled for his life.

During the month that followed, Bambi came into the house only after making sure once he entered that Nonny wasn't around. But a month later, after Nonny attacked him once again, Bambi never tried to come into the house again. The relationship between Nonny and Bambi in the yard also suffered. Bambi hid all the time, ate leftovers, and had to sneak over to one of the cat houses for quick naps at night. Finally he'd had enough of this refugee lifestyle, and one sunny morning he suddenly appeared again at the front entrance. He came inside courageously and explored extensively. Then he came back to me and asked to be let out. When he left, he turned his heard toward me and I could see in his eyes that he was saying goodbye and embarking on a new life. I told my husband and he laughed at me, saying I was imagining things and that I couldn't possibly read the mind of a cat. He should have realized by then that I had a special rapport with my cats. In any case, this time I hoped he was right and I was wrong, because Bambi was a good-natured and beautiful cat, and it was hard for me to think of the community without him. But it turned out that I was right; Bambi disappeared.

Bambi

Six months later Bambi suddenly reappeared in the garden. He looked like he had been doing well, though he was a little thin. Nonny was on one of his long walks and Bambi took advantage of the situation and stayed in the yard for several days, eating well and sleeping. He no longer asked to be let in the house.

The female cats recognized Bambi and didn't try to drive him away. The males in the garden were all young, and Bambi established a peaceful coexistence with them as well. Then one night, about a week later, Bambi disappeared, this time without saying goodbye. In the morning when I went out to feed the cats, Bambi simply wasn't there. He never reappeared after that, nor did I ever see him in another yard or neighborhood.

Furry's fate wasn't much better than Bambi's. Although Nonny attacked Bambi first and continued to allow Furry to lie in the living room for a few more weeks, their story had the same ending. One bright day when Furry was lying on the sofa, Nonny came in, and without any warning he jumped on the sofa and attacked Furry just as he had done with Bambi. Furry, who was a lazy and spoiled cat, cried out in terror and his yelps pierced my heart. He tried to roll over on his back to let Nonny know that he had surrendered and that there was no need to continue attacking him. However, Nonny didn't let him go and dragged him toward the entrance, where he must have bit him quite seriously because Furry shrieked in terror one more time and then disappeared.

Unlike Bambi, Furry never dared enter the house again. He was also afraid to stay in the garden. Probably no more than a couple of days later I went out into the garden and Furry came over, rubbed up against me, and when I sat in one of the wicker armchairs he jumped on me and I suddenly realized that he was saying goodbye. And that was that. Furry left and never returned.

I mourned Furry's departure and missed his physical presence. There was no one to sit on my lap as I read a book or watched television. I was therefore delighted when fate brought us together one more time.

One day, months after Furry had left, I was driving home from the university through a neighborhood called Givat HaMivtar, when all of a sudden I caught sight of a handsome cat, the spitting image of Furry, sitting on the steps of an elegant house. Since there are always a few Furries around, I wasn't at all sure that this was my Furry, especially since Givat HaMivtar is quite far from my house in Beit HaKerem. How could he have gotten there? I decided to check anyway. I parked the car in the first empty spot I found. I got out and walked back to where I had seen the cat, which was still there. The moment he saw me he started running toward me. I bent down and he jumped into my arms. It was indeed my Furry! He was wearing a stylish collar and a flea collar, and he looked simply amazing. His owners had even dyed two locks of his fur purple. I didn't like this addition, but it showed that his owners were proud of his beauty. As I was crouching down with Furry in my arms, I wondered how I could find out who his owners were and how he had come to live with them.

I would be lying if I didn't admit to a having had the sinful thought of taking Furry back to my car and bringing him home. I certainly thought about it and I probably would have done it if I hadn't known that Furry wasn't safe with me. Even if he were neutered, Nonny would not tolerate Furry in his territory and certainly not in the house.

While Furry and I were enjoying our reunion, a sweet girl who was about twelve years old walked over to us and in an excited voice asked why I was holding her cat. I told her that Furry was born and raised in my garden and that one day he disappeared after being driven away by the male leader of my community when he reached adulthood. I asked her how they had come to have Furry; she hesitated and said that her mother, who was home, would tell me. I was invited inside, and with Furry still in my arms I entered the pleasant, neat house. A woman with a welcoming countenance opened the door for us, and her daughter excitedly recounted what I had just told her.

The woman, whose name was Dana, told me how Furry had come to stay with them. A few months ago, she said, she and her husband went to visit friends who lived on a street very close to mine, and they saw Furry. When their friends saw them admiring Furry, the friends explained that they couldn't adopt him because they had a dog that didn't get along with cats, so they made do with feeding him and providing a box with a blanket for him in their stairwell. They said that Furry had appeared in their garden one sunny day looking hungry and tired. They suspected that he had had a home, and that something must have happened to cause him to leave. Dana and her husband, Avner, asked their friends if they could adopt Furry as their pet. The proposal was happily accepted. Since that day, Furry has lived in their house and they have loved him and taken exemplary care of him. Dana apologized a bit for the purple strands of fur and said that it was their daughter, Maya, and her brother, Tomer, who came up with the idea.

Over coffee I told Dana and Maya Furry's story, and how happy I was to see him doing so well. With trepidation Dana asked me whether I wanted to take Furry back, and I replied that even if I wanted to, it would be impossible due to Nonny's aggression. I also added that knowing Furry had a good home was enough for me. The mother and daughter breathed a sigh of relief. It was obvious they truly loved the cat.

After about an hour and a half I said goodbye to the threesome, but not before we exchanged numbers and addresses. As I was leaving, Maya asked us who we thought Furry would choose to live with if he had the choice. I told her I didn't know if Furry would be willing to give up his current home, but that emotionally I thought he was very attached to me because I helped raise him since the day he was born. Dana suggested we test this. They would stand at just inside the front door, leaving it open, and I would walk through it. By seeing if Furry chose to stay inside with them or follow me, we would have our answer.

Readers can guess what happened. Furry didn't hesitate for a second. The moment I started walking away, he quickly ran after me. He walked beside me to the car and it was clear that he wanted to jump in. I bent down, picked him up, and called for Maya. When Maya ran up beside us, I placed Furry in her arms, where he stayed, and I got into the car and drove away.

Ever since that day I call Furry's family once a week and visit him twice a year. Furry is already eleven years old and he is still as alert, kind, sensitive, and spoiled as ever.

Following the birth of the first Furry and Bambi, quite a few other Furries were born in the yard. At first glance, they all resembled each other in color and their long fur. But those who knew them had no problem distinguishing between them. It was easy to identify unique physical features like the appearance of a sudden white patch in a tortoiseshell coat, or the presence of a dominant light brown color. A cat's size also helps identify it. The most important features, however, are a cat's face and character. On several occasions I had two Furries at that same time that looked exactly the same. Even their faces and the way they swung their tails were similar from time to time, which meant I could only tell them apart by their behavior. Furries were usually extremely patient, calm, and laid-back. They wouldn't be seen scurrying to a plate of food. Instead they waited patiently off to one side for a particular cat to finish eating so they could take its place. Furries could usually be found sunbathing for long periods of time. They were much more likely to enjoy being petted than other cats. Even the females liked being petted, not just the males, and they didn't run away quickly when a stranger appeared. Males reached sexual maturity a little later than other cats, as did females.

Unfortunately, these same traits mean that Furries were more susceptible to being run over by a car due to the deliberate pace at which they crossed the road. They were also more vulnerable to disease. I don't know why, but perhaps grooming their long fur caused them to occasionally swallow hairballs, which then caused digestive problems that might have resulted in a general weakness that rendered these cats even more sensitive to disease.

In any case, many Furries did not survive beyond two years of age. So the birth of a Furry was always accompanied with some trepidation on my part. And it was sad. It was so sad to sit next to these beautiful kittens, pet them, feed them, and worry about what would happen to them. I always tried to find homes for Furries. Fortunately their beauty led to me managing to arrange quite a few adoptions.

As I'm writing this book, there are two, sometimes three Furries in the yard during the main meal of the day. One female that usually appears and waits in a corner while the other cats devour the food has an almost uniform brownish gray color. She was born in my yard and stayed with her brother, the only two cats from their litter to survive. Their mother, an ordinary tabby from Kitsushi's family, disappeared into another garden when the two kittens were quite small, so from a very early age I fed them. The male kitten is a regular tabby. The female Furry tended to sleep a lot as a kitten and was rather apathetic, while her sibling was full of life. He constantly tried to play with her, but she would quickly quit their games in order to take a nap. Her frustrated brother couldn't find other playmates (at that time there were no small kittens in the yard), so he came up with a series of one-player games, which he seemed to enjoy. The little tabby learned to amuse himself and I would watch him from the large living room window, which faced the cat pergola, and see how he turned every blade of grass into a challenging game. I loved him. He was a cat after my own heart: friendly, resourceful, and energetic. And because I was touched by his loneliness, I would sometimes go out to the cat pergola and the yard to play with him.

The owner of the pet store sometime sent me different feathered and mouse-shaped animal toys as a complementary gift along with the cats' food. I usually didn't give the toys to the cats because some of them seemed dangerous. As readers will see in a later chapter, I learned the hard way that these toys can indeed cause serious problems. A kitten, and even an adult cat, might swallow bits of feather, or catch its leg in the elastic string attached to a mouse-shaped woolen stuffed animal, for example. I would therefore go outside with a toy or two, play with the tabby for half an hour, and at the end of the game take the toys with me and store them where the cats couldn't reach them. On rare occasions we were joined by his sister in our play, but only for a short time.

For some reason I never named these two cats and simply called them the female Furry and the tabby. When I saw how they developed, I was certain that the female Furry with her low energy level would not last, while the tabby would grow into a magnificent male cat. Sometimes I thought that he might be lucky enough to become the leader of the community and wouldn't be forced to leave my territory.

During the first year and a half of their lives, it seemed that my predictions were coming true, at least as far as the tabby was concerned. He grew into a big cat and he didn't let the leader at the time, Stripy, chase him away from the territory. The female Furry managed to give birth once before we caught her and spayed her. The kittens all died shortly after they were born.

As we know, the world is full of surprises, both good and bad. The tabby continued to grow and became a very impressive cat, but he did not live past his second year. He must have been hit by a car while crossing the road. He managed to return to the cat pergola and get into one of the beds, where I found him, lifeless.

The female Furry, on the other hand, became a bit more energetic after being spayed and she still shows up for meals and sometimes makes an appearance near the front entrance as if to announce that this is her home. I have no idea which garden she occupies or where she sleeps during the cold winter nights. Every morning when I see her, I am happy all over again. I hope that she'll continue to stick around for a very long time.

This story relates to my anxieties about the cats. When one takes care of street cats and has no way to control their behavior in the street or where they sleep—assuming they choose not to sleep in the beds provided—there is the constant fear that this might be the last time one sees a particular cat. It is therefore quite an emotional burden to take care of twenty street cats, and it is difficult to describe the hours, which I'm sure add up to days and weeks, my heart has ached with fear for the fate of a certain cat. In fact, peaceful periods without a minor or major tragedy are actually quite rare.

The second Furry that appears for breakfast is different from all the others. It arrived at the cat pergola one sunny day at the age of about six months. Touching this cat is out of the question, and because of its long hair, I can't determine whether it's a male or a female or whether the cat has been fixed. In any case, during the months it stayed in the yard, the cat did not get pregnant or court any females during mating season, nor did I hear any courting songs. Its gender remains a mystery. Who knows, perhaps one day I will find out the second Furry's gender.

the ginger Furry

The third Furry is a female cat that was born in my yard. I never named her either. I call her the ginger Furry to distinguish her from the brownish gray one. She has also been spayed and she is now seven or eight years old. Lately she hardly comes to the main meals, and a few days ago I saw her on the street looking unwell. She meowed when she saw me—something she's never done before—and her paws weren't clean. From experience I've learned that when a cat stops being meticulous about grooming, its health is in decline. I was greatly saddened to see her in this condition and I ran home and brought out some food for her. She ate ravenously, another ominous sign since when a cat eats like this it is often an indication that the cat senses its poor health and eats like its starving in a desperate attempt to get better.

A few days have passed since I last saw her on the street and this morning she appeared for a meal and her paws seemed cleaner to me. Who knows, her health might be improving. Naturally I am anxious for her.

And that's the story of the Furries to this day. Now back to the Bambies. Bambies are rare in my neighborhood. Only three other Bambies have been born since the original Bambi. A Bambi, let me remind you, is a cat whose coat is gray all over with the exception of its four white feet.

Only one of the Bambies stayed in my territory. He remained for three years after he was born, and recently he's moved to another yard where there is thick undergrowth. Sometimes I see him walking leisurely and contentedly along a path near some buildings at the end of our street. Other times I see him in the cat pergola, checking to see if I left a big bowl of dry cat food outside. Only rarely does he appear for the big meal of the day.

The other Bambies followed the same path as the original Bambi. Both were males and when they reached sexual maturity, the leader of the community drove them out of the territory.

One interesting fact, though it's purely a matter of chance, is that two of the three Bambies lost an eye as small kittens as a result of a serious infection that no antibiotics or cream that I administered could cure. Both of them managed quite well with one eye, and the Bambi that remained in my territory fared just fine. I can only hope that the one that was banished from my territory is living a decent life elsewhere.

Chapter 9: The Silver Cat

In one of Big Mama's litters there were two gorgeous kittens: the first was Sophie, whose story has already been told, and the second was her brother, whom I called Silver since his coat was actually silver rather than gray. As six-month-old kittens, both of them used to sit on the roof of my car that was parked near our home. Sometimes, when I went outside, I would see mothers and their children pointing at those two particularly beautiful and special kittens.

Silver

Unlike Sophie, Silver didn't sleep in the garden. He found himself a nice little spot in the stairwell of the house across from ours. The woman who lived on the main floor was an avid cat lover and she also regularly fed street cats. In winter she put a blanket for Silver in the corner that he made his own, and she loved him just as much as I did.

He visited my garden for all three meals by jumping from the road onto a high fence and from there into the yard. My cats accepted him with love, and the females could even be seen flirting with him. Silver enjoyed the attention he got and the food he ate at my place, and he often stayed in the yard between meals. He bonded with the other cats and spent his time lying in the sun or playing mock battle games with kittens that were more or less his age.

He and his sister were close. When Sophie had her accident and lay for in the cat pergola for a long time, it was Silver who came to visit her several times a day. He was the only cat that dared approach her. She drove away all the other cats that tried. She emitted threatening sounds and the curious visitors quickly ran away.

When Sophie first gave birth and brought her kittens to the basement next to the pergola, Silver was the only cat that dared go down into the basement to see his nephews and nieces. He also played a lot with kittens from her more successful litters.

When Silver grew up and was one year old, I expected him to be driven out of the garden now that he was sexually mature and Stripy couldn't tolerate any handsome adult male hanging around and possibly competing with him. But nothing of the sort happened. Moreover, when mating season arrived, Silver remained indifferent to the hullabaloo around him. Silver continued to be sexually indifferent until he was two years old, which meant that he could remain at home in the yard.

As I've mentioned, Silver was a respected and beloved member of the community. Silver was particularly helpful toward kittens that tested their strength by climbing on the roof of the pergola and got stuck there.

Until Silver took on the role of stranded kitten rescuer, the task had fallen on me. I hated this job, since my tools for getting the kittens down from the roof of the pergola were quite limited. From below, I could raise a broom toward the kitten, which it could have used to climb down if only it could be made to understand. I could also stand on the ground with a large basket padded with rags into which the kitten could jump. With great effort I could even attach the basket to the end of the broom and reach this contraption toward the kitten, but the kitten would still be almost a foot above the basket and I had to try to coax him to jump into it.

All the kittens hated way I tried to rescue them from the roof. They refused to make use of the broom and the basket, and perhaps they were right. I only ever convinced a kitten to use the basket once. I told the story of this first success, and the second attempt resulted in the basket flipping over and the kitten dropped to the ground, miraculously unhurt.

Silver, on the other hand, would go up to the pergola and show the kitten by example which branch to use to cross from the roof to a tree in the least scary way. Afterward he would show the kitten how to descend, and which branches to use to reach the ground safely.

In this way, Silver managed to coax down quite a few scared kittens. The problem was when a kitten was stranded on the roof of the pergola and Silver wasn't in the yard. I would run to the neighbor's house to check if Silver was in his regular sleeping spot or in the nearby garden. When I managed to find him, I would call him, using sounds, pantomime, and speech, and explain that his presence was required in the yard. I think that the sounds and pantomime were redundant. It was as if Silver understood what I was saying because he always—yes, always—accompanied me immediately.

When Silver was two and a half years old and still didn't appear to be interested in females, I suddenly realized that he was losing his appetite. Things became so serious that he would come to breakfast, smell the food, and leave. I started worrying that he was sick, because as readers have seen, bad surprises are commonplace when it comes to street cats. Silver began missing meals and my anxiety mounted.

This strange behavior lasted for three weeks, and then Silver disappeared for three days. When he returned, he looked to be doing well and seemed to be full of life, though skinner than he had been. There were two reasonable explanations: either Silver had discovered the allure of the "great cat outdoors" and went exploring in unfamiliar territories, or he had become a mature cat and was exploring to see if he could find a community that he could join with females to his liking. I hope that the latter was the case, because after he returned from two brief explorations, Silver went out on one more walk and I never saw him again on our street.

I believe that Silver's unique character made it impossible for him feel sexually attracted to the cats he had grown up with for two and a half years, treating them like sisters.

I am confident of one thing, though. It doesn't matter where Silver settled after he left us. Given his extraordinary beauty and easygoing nature, there are probably people taking care of him, wherever he decided to make his home.

The entire community mourned Silver's departure. Sophie in particular felt his absence. She became depressed and for several days she slept most of the time, skipping most meals.

But life goes on and Sophie became her old self again. The community got used to living without Silver, but both the cats and I miss him to this day.

Chapter 10:
Grayush: The Pavarotti of Cats

About ten years ago, right after our pergola and the cat pergola were built, Little Mama gave birth in one of the neighborhood gardens. A week later, Little Mama moved the four kittens that had survived into our famous basement with a door opening onto the cat pergola. As I've already described, the basement is located about five feet underground, so the kittens were safely hidden deep in the earth. Just to remind readers, the basement door is usually closed but not locked. To get her kittens down the hole, a mother had to push the door firmly with her front legs or her entire body, and this was probably what Little Mama did. Afterward, in order

Little Mama

to nurse the kittens, the mother needs to go down into the basement herself, stay there with the kittens, and then emerge from the basement to get a breath of fresh air.

I found out that there were kittens in the basement when I heard cries emerge from its depths one morning. I went outside and saw that the basement door was a little ajar and I immediately moved away. I didn't want to fling open the door to see who was there lest I frighten the mother and her kittens. At first I didn't know who the mother was, but after waiting patiently beside the large window facing the cat pergola, I saw Little Mama jump into the basement.

I was relieved because Little Mama was one of the rare females that let me touch her and didn't run away. I thought that if she were to need help with the kittens, she would cooperate. For three weeks, it was business as usual: Little Mama went down into the basement several times a day, fed and bathed the kittens, and later she went up to the cat pergola and lay in one of the cat beds or in the sun, where she had clear sight of the basement.

However, it seemed that feeding four kittens was hard for Little Mama, because after three weeks I began to hear cries once again emerge from the basement. This time the cries didn't stop. I went outside to see what was happening and saw Little Mama lying in the sun, ignoring the cries. I gathered my courage and opened the basement door. Little Mama didn't move an inch. I took one more step and climbed down into the basement. I was greeted by the sight of a bundle of four kittens lying on top of each other. I picked them up and examined each kitten. They didn't appear to be sick, but they were very small. I climbed out of the basement, brought up one kitten after another, and fed them outside. At such a young age, they ate baby formula and a little bit of special meat I prepared for kittens.

When I finished feeding the four kittens for the first time, Little Mama came over and rubbed up against me, as if in gratitude. I stroked her a few times and then she jumped back into the basement, carried her kittens back into their dark home, and stayed with them down there for quite some time.

And so, for the next few weeks, Little Mama and I continued the joint task of feeding the kittens. I fed them outside because I wanted to bring them out of the darkness, but each time Little Mama brought them back down into the basement. I waited for Little Mama to decide that it was time for them to emerge once and for all. The kittens remained small and weren't yet big enough to be inoculated.

One morning, when I went down into the basement to bring the kittens up for their meal—by now they were eating more of the special meat I prepared—I saw that two of them were suffering from eye infections. From experience, I knew that Little Mama and I, not to mentioned the kittens, were heading for trouble.

And so the routine continued. Every day, three times a day, I fed and administered medicine to the four kittens. Finally, I decided that the dark basement wasn't doing them any good and I took the initiative to bring the four kittens into the cat pergola and firmly shut the basement door so Little Mama wouldn't be able to bring them back down into the darkness. The kittens remained outside and the sun helped at least two of them; they started showing signs of improvement. Their eyes opened, they ate more, and they even began to play. The other two, the weakest of the four, slowly faded away despite all my efforts. I couldn't save them.

With two kittens left, one gray all over and the other a tabby, Little Mama redoubled her efforts to care for them. They were still nursing, but they received most of their food from me. When they were three months old the tabby vanished, no one knows where. Only the gray kitten remained. Grayush grew and developed but remained a relatively small cat. He suffered almost

Grayush

every possible affliction. One time he developed a rash and his whole body was covered with sores, which remained with him throughout most of his nine years. The sores would disappear for a while and then return. As he grew older, the sores appeared less frequently. Grayush also developed allergic rhinitis. He would constantly sneeze and he suffered from a runny nose and sometimes a cough. The amount of medicine that Grayush consumed during the nine years he lived was greater than the total amount of medicine I gave all the other cats in my community.

To put it bluntly, in addition to being weak Grayush was a decidedly unattractive male. I didn't foresee any brilliant future for him, but I hoped that the leader of the community wouldn't view him as a threat and would refrain from chasing him away. And that's just what happened; Grayush remained a permanent resident in the cat pergola and in the yard.

One night, when he was three years old, I heard magnificent singing coming from the yard. It took me a moment or two to realize that this was a cat's mating call. Until that evening, I had never heard such singing before, and no other cat has managed to sing so beautifully since. I tried to guess which cat possessed this fantastic talent. Only a few days later, when I saw Grayush sitting on a tree branch producing melodious sounds, did I realize that this beloved cat of mine, despite and perhaps because he was so wretched, was in fact not miserable at all! As readers probably know, mating calls are extremely significant for females being courted. They also matter greatly when a male faces another male to fight for a desired female.

What Grayush lacked in appearance, he made up for with his magnificent singing. The result was that after Stripy's reign as leader of the community ended, Grayush became the leader and held the post for two years. The cats preferred him to a large and beautiful male that came from outside the community and wanted to take on the leadership after Stripy passed away. Grayush did nothing but raise his voice in song. After he did that a few times, the strange cat gave up and left the stage to Grayush. All the residents of the yard— the older females, the kittens, and the young males that made up the leader's "warm-up act"— accepted Grayush's leadership with love. It was clear that his voice cast a spell over them all. Since Grayush wasn't at all violent, his leadership was the most peaceful reign the community had ever experienced. Cats from outside the community that tried to usurp his place gave up once they heard him sing. Sometimes the entire community would sit and listen to Grayush vocalize and sing.

Grayush guided the community's life peacefully, cooperating fully with me. Our relationship, which we'd had since his kittenhood, remained very close. He came to me every morning when I went out into the yard, and he let me know if there was a problem with one of the cats—for example, if a cat had been in an accident, or if there was a new litter and the mother couldn't find a good spot for them. Grayush had various methods of letting me know when problems arose. Either he would lead me to the problem, like a sick kitten, or he would stand next to the problem, such as a new litter or a confused mother, and emit special sounds and make sure I came over. Afterward getting my attention he wouldn't leave my side until I adequately addressed the problem. In this way from a weak and incredibly ugly cat there arose an intelligent and empathic leader.

There were many things that Grayush learned on his own, likely because he had been alone for most of his kittenhood. He learned to keep himself entertained by acquiring new skills. For example, when he was little, he didn't join the gang that tried to learn how to climb up onto the roof of the pergola. But when he was one year old, he tested his strength by climbing up the tree next to the pergola and then jumped from the tree to the roof of the pergola. The climb was the relatively easy part for him, as it was for most cats. The problem, as I've said before, was getting down from the roof, because the only way to do so was while facing down and not being able to judge the distance to the ground below. Grayush tried to gather his courage and jump from the roof to the tree. He assumed a jumping position several times, and at the very last minute he got spooked and changed his mind. He began investigating other possibilities and decided that it might be possible to get down from the pergola without looking down by using the wooden beams that were part of the pergola walls. As readers have seen, many cats used this method. He began descending backward until he finally reached the ground, trembling with fear. The next day he successfully climbed up to the roof again, and once more tried to gather his courage to descend via the tree. But he got spooked again. Since I knew from the previous day that he had an alternative way down, I didn't worry that he would be stranded on the roof for long. Indeed, once he realized that he still wasn't brave enough to descend in a way befitting a cat, as was the method employed by many cats in the yard, he once again used the beams to get down. The story repeated itself daily and I often got to see how Grayush tried to overcome his fear and jump to the tree but balked at the last moment.

One day I was sitting in the study next to the kitchen when I heard strange and unfamiliar cries. I immediately ran to the large window overlooking the cat pergola. I saw Grayush sitting in a tree facing down and his tail held high. I realized that he had finally found his courage and jumped into the tree. He lingered there only to let everyone know that he had succeeded. This was before he started singing with his amazing voice. But the sounds that came out of his moth were cries of joy or victory and they were also pleasing to the ear.

In time, when Grayush became the leader, he taught the art of climbing to kittens that struggled to climb onto the roof of the pergola, and particularly those who struggled to climb back down. I noticed that he always taught them both methods of descent.

Grayush was also a different leader from his predecessor when it came to feeding arrangements. He was more like Nonny, who personally took care of kittens during mealtimes. Grayush helped weak cats reach food first. He did this in his own gentle and considerate way. He would walk with a weak or scared kitten toward one of the plates, and with determination, but without any violence, he would push away a big fat cat from its spot near the plate and make room for the weakling.

It was evident that Grayush remembered his own hardships as a lonely kitten and whenever he saw a cat standing by itself in the yard or in the cat pergola, he would approach it and start to play. More than once, I saw Grayush running around with a kitten in search of a beetle or a lizard as he encouraged the kitten to try to catch the bug. They wouldn't kill it, but play with it as if it were a ball.

Grayush kept his position as leader for two years until he was seven years old. Afterward he decided for himself that being a leader was too difficult for him. His colds became more frequent and he often required medical attention and several days in a warm bed to recuperate.

Leo

With grace, he simply stepped down from his role as the leader of the community.

But since Grayush continued to sing magnificently even though he was no longer the leader, a few months passed before another cat dared take up his position. His successor was a male from a nearby territory that looked like a lion, hence his name, Leo.

For two more years, Grayush continued to live a comfortable and pleasant life. Leo treated him with respect, and he was surrounded by adult cats and kittens that loved him and frequently rubbed up against him. During those years he became close friends with Beauty and Colomina, cats that, like him, were also in retirement: him from his role as leader and them from their role as mothers. It was touching to see two or three of my "old folks" rubbing against each other in the sun, accompanying one another along the path leading to nearby houses, or eating together from the same plate.

It was the first time my female cats stopped giving birth because of old age rather than disease, an accident, or being spayed. And it was also the first time a leader of the community continued to live there after his term had ended. Because they were retired, the friendship between these three cats was very special and contained elements of shared idleness and mutual assistance, like guarding food.

I witnessed a similar friendship between old cats only between Kitsushi and Geezer. As I mentioned, Kitsushi left the territory once she stopped giving birth and Geezer left with her, or so I guessed, because he disappeared and made way for Nonny. Two years after the couple left I saw them together in the beautiful garden of close friends of mine. It turned out that I was right and the two had chosen to grow old together. It was such a touching sight that even my husband, who rarely shows emotion, was moved. Geezer looked sick and weak and Kitsushi hadn't changed a bit. When they came to me as adults, I had no idea how old they were, but it was clear to me that Geezer was at least ten years old.

The following summer Geezer's body was discovered in one of my neighbor's gardens. The municipal veterinarian who came to examine the body said that he had died of old age. As I've already mentioned, I continued to see Kitsushi by herself in my friends' garden until she disappeared.

When Grayush was nine years old, he suffered from a running nose and began coughing quite frequently. No medicine could cure him, and his stomach became strangely bloated.

When the cat catcher came around to trap cats to be neutered or spayed, I asked him to catch Grayush and to have him examined at the animal hospital, not neutered. Grayush was examined and I was told that his overall condition wasn't too bad given his age, but that his runny nose had become chronic and couldn't be treated. As for the swelling in his stomach, I was told the tests that they'd managed to run showed nothing. But Grayush's condition worsened and his stomach became so distended that he looked pregnant.

I faced a difficult dilemma. Should I take Grayush to the vet once more to have him thoroughly examined, or let him live out the remainder of his days in his territory? It was a hard decision to make. Despite what I'd been told by the animal hospital, my conscience wouldn't rest and kept bugging me to bring Grayush to the veterinarian again.

To this day I still don't know whether I made the right decision or not, but Grayush helped me make it. In spite of his runny nose and bloated stomach, he continued to live a regular life. He ran and jumped, which made me put off the visit to the veterinarian.

And then, all at once, I saw that Grayush stopped jumping onto tall objects and that he was having a hard time jumping over the fence in the yard. He also started drinking a lot. It seemed to me that his condition was deteriorating by the day. I could no longer hesitate. I took the cage and without a fuss put Grayush inside it. He was simply too weak and powerless to resist. I drove with him straight to our relatively new veterinarian, the one who didn't put animals to sleep unless he was convinced that they were beyond saving. He examined Grayush and determined that the cat should be left at the clinic to undergo more thorough tests.

Grayush remained there for more tests and after a few days, the veterinarian called to say that Grayush's kidneys were damaged. This meant that he could only live for an indefinite period of time in a cage while connected to an IV. There was no way to manage the condition, let alone cure it. It wasn't clear how long he would live in the cage. I looked at Grayush, who at nine and a half years of age found himself in a cage with an IV. I saw a cat dejected by his situation. Again I didn't know what to do. Should I prolong his life, though it wasn't clear for how long—probably days, or at best, weeks—by keeping him locked up in a cage and hooked to an IV in a strange place, or should I end his suffering?

The veterinarian didn't interfere. He waited while I sat down and thought. In truth, my reasoning was quite simple. If I were Grayush, what would I prefer: to die in my sleep or to live as in invalid in pain and discomfort in a cage, away from nature?

I made the decision for Grayush, and with all my heart I hope that I made the right choice. I asked the vet to put him to sleep. I stroked Grayush, the ugliest and most charming of cats, one last time before he was given an injection to render him unconscious before the lethal injection was administered.

With a heavy heart, I drove back home. The entrance, my parking space (where Grayush spent many hours sitting on the roof of my car), and the yard seemed empty to me. I couldn't stand being home and I fled the house and roamed the streets.

I walked along the streets in my neighborhood with tears streaming down my face, and I kept thinking how difficult it was to feed and care for more than twenty cats. One has to go through so many tragedies, both large and small, when caring for street cats. And then I remembered Grayush singing in his magnificent voice and I began to smile as I cried. I forced myself to remember that Grayush had had a good life and knew how to enjoy every second of it. The pain remained, but with it were all the good memories that made me feel that caring for street cats was indeed a worthy moral endeavor and that as such it was no wonder that it was not only wondrous and amazing, but also difficult and exhausting.

Chapter 11: A Short but Happy Life

Tete the Duchess

Tete wasn't born in my garden. Her mother was Colomina, who brought her to our front door when she was three months old, along with three other kittens. Right from the start, Tete stood out because of her beauty.

Tete

She was part of the group of cats I named the Furries, but she possessed an additional magnificence about her. The fur around her neck created a sort of luxurious collar and her general shape and gray-brown coloring were very dignified. Even as a kitten, her gait was regal.

When Tete arrived in the garden with her siblings, I looked at her (I guessed that she was a female from the shape of her face) and wondered how she would fit in with my community full of commoners. Though there were some very beautiful cats, none were as majestic as she was.

I was sure that she wouldn't let me touch her, but I went over to her and tried. I extended my hand toward her and she didn't run away. On the contrary, she came even closer. I took a chance and petted her and she purred contentedly. I sat in one of the wicker armchairs and to my amazement, this majestic cat leaped straight onto my lap. We remained sitting like that for a while; I petted her in amazement and she remained curled up on my lap.

When I got up to feed the cats, it wasn't clear to me how she would get along with everyone else given her unique character. To my delight, they welcomed her and her three siblings and she easily found a place at one of the plates.

Unlike Colomina's other kittens, which did not settle in the garden and visited only for meals, Tete became a full member of the community. She quickly found a cat house for herself. There were several empty cat houses during those sunny days. She played with the kittens that had been born in the yard and it always seemed to me that they treated her with respect, as if she really were Her Royal Highness the Duchess Tete.

Months went by and Tete reached sexual maturity. This was before I began neutering and spaying the cats in the community. Tete became pregnant and after three weeks it became clear that her health was suffering. I went out into the garden for a few hours to see exactly what was happening with her and quickly discovered that she was barely eating, but she was drinking enormous quantities of water and urinating quite frequently.

I placed Tete in a cage, called the vet, and soon afterward, we were on our way to see him. Tete remained with the vet overnight for various tests. The next day, when I came to take her home, the veterinarian told me that Tete was suffering from diabetes—not the ordinary kind, mind you, but diabetes insipidus, which in Tete's case involved the pituitary gland.

Tete underwent surgery to remove her fetuses and returned home. Due to the special diet she was required to follow, she clearly couldn't remain in the garden. She had to become a full-fledged house cat. Since Nonny stayed in the basement where he had his armchair, bed, and litter box, Tete needed her own space. She herself chose one of the armchairs in the living room as her bed and I "sacrificed" the guest bathroom, which was right near the front entrance, for her litter box. At that time, I was living alone and willing to give up my comfort for Tete's sake.

After trying to escape for several days, Tete eventually got used to her new situation. To her credit, I can say that she didn't disrupt life inside the house. She also didn't scratch the furniture or rugs. Like Nonny, she simply made herself at home and I barely noticed her presence. She received two meals a day. Nonny didn't try to eat from her plate and she didn't come close to his. While Nonny was home, the two of them lived in peaceful coexistence. Though they never played together, they also weren't envious of each other and never fought for my attention.

When friends came over, Nonny usually ignored the company, but Tete enjoyed the attention and universal praise and let my guests play with her. I brought home a few harmless toys, such as a little ball and a mouse-shaped toy, and Tete amused herself with them. When I was home, she always followed me around the house, though she never slept in my bed. I believe she must have slept while I wasn't home, because whenever I returned she was always in her armchair.

This was a new experience for me. Even though I had taken care of numerous cats, I had never had a proper house cat apart from the brief time Shushka lived indoors. Nonny wasn't really a house cat since he spent more time outside than inside.

I came to love Tete's presence in the house and whenever I returned home, I immediately called her name, and if she weren't in a deep sleep she would immediately run to me. In the evenings when I stayed in, we would spend hours together listening to music or watching television, with Tete frequently curled up on my lap like a typical house cat. I had a feeling that Tete understood what was happening on television, for when I turned on the TV, she would sit and gaze at it, utterly fascinated. When I chose to read, Tete sat beside me rather than on my lap so as not to disturb my reading. She simply adapted herself to me. During our numerous games she always managed to avoid scratching me. She didn't even shed.

The only thing that cast a shadow over Tete's presence was her health. The veterinarian wasn't convinced that she didn't have a brain tumor that was causing the excessive drinking, and he warned me that despite strictly following her diet, Tete's condition could suddenly deteriorate.

When Tete reached a year old, I calmed down a little and thought that the worst was behind us and that this wonderful, loving cat would make it. Our happiness continued for six more months; Tete flourished and our relationship deepened.

After a while, I noticed that Tete started drinking large quantities of water again and was frequently going to the litter box.

I immediately called the veterinarian and he suggested that I go to the animal hospital. I followed his advice and Tete underwent an extensive examination. The veterinarians concluded that there was indeed a brain tumor and that it was possible to try to operate to remove it, but the location of the tumor was problematic and it wasn't clear how Tete would fare after it was removed. She might be partially paralyzed. The alternative was to put her on medication, which would slow down the progression of the disease a little and prolong her life. Without hesitation I chose the latter option. For about three months, there was some improvement in Tete's condition. Unfortunately, it didn't last and her health began to deteriorate once more. This time there was no other choice and I decided that Tete should undergo surgery.

During those last few moments before she was anesthetized, I stroked her and kissed her, trying not cry to avoid causing her any distress. I said goodbye to her and knew that I would never see her again. I had a premonition about what was to come. The surgery turned out the be extremely complicated. The doctors were competent; the fault was with the cruelty of nature putting the tumor in such a difficult spot.

Tete never woke up. I entrusted a good friend to see to her burial somewhere in nature. I didn't have the mental strength to bury Tete.

Thus my duchess left me, the only full-time house cat that I've ever had. Luckily Nonny returned home now and then, but most of the time I felt an oppressive loneliness. I missed Tete's constant presence terribly. But just as I have never adopted another dog after losing my beloved dog Kato, I also didn't bring another cat into my home. I wasn't missing a cat. I was missing Tete.

A Cat Named Legs

Little Mama's last litter before she disappeared included only tabbies. One tabby had a white stomach and white legs, and soon after Little Mama brought him to the garden with the rest of the kittens, I named him Legs.

His legs were indeed long and beautiful, and like all males, perhaps even more so than most, he was a friendly and loving cat. He always accompanied me when I went out into the garden and preferred walking beside me to running straight for the plates of food. Only after I put down all the plates would Legs find a spot for himself.

Legs

He was also an incredibly smart cat. As a kitten he would often surprise me with the kinds of new games that he played, and he also involved his siblings and a few other kittens from another litter that were in garden at the time. He invented a game of hide-and-seek. Incredible as this might sound, Legs taught the other kittens to play hide-and-seek. He taught them to stay put, to not look where he was going, and only after allowing a short amount of time to pass—time he used to hide behind a leafy branch, or in one of the closed cat houses, or behind the air conditioning unit that was located outside the house—would the kittens start running around the garden searching for him.

The first time I saw all the kittens standing still and Legs running and hiding, I didn't exactly understand what was happening. I decided to stay in the garden for a while longer every day until I figured it out. This is how I discovered that this was indeed a game of hide-and-seek. My cat-loving friends were incredulous and I suggested they come over and see the game with their own eyes. Legs chose to play hide-and-seek after dinner, at dusk, so two friends were able to witness the game as it was taking place.

In addition, Legs was an excellent climber, just like Sophie. He was the only cat that as a kitten dared climb one of the cypress trees in the garden and managed to get down without a problem. This accomplishment was the result of days of practice. Every day he would climb another branch and then climb down. In this way, he learned not to fear the descent and didn't panic when he looked down from his perch up in the tree. When he was small, he climbed on the pergola using the wooden beams. Only later did he begin to climb using the tree next to the pergola.

One could say that Legs believed in learning by trying. Getting out of the garden was another thing that he learned gradually. At first, he would exit through the opening in the fence that I created for kittens and the less talented adult climbers to access the garden. Later he watched a particular Furry female that was an excellent climber and saw how she leaped onto the fence and balanced as only cats can, and from the fence, how she jumped outside.

Legs loved walking and in particular crossing roads. He even understood the danger of cars. He would listen and look to his right and then to his left—yes, he actually looked both ways before crossing the street. That was extraordinary. Most cats can't comprehend the danger posed by cars, even though they sometimes see other cats get run over right in front of their eyes!

I want to reiterate a sensitive topic that I believe needs repeating—the prevalence of cats hit by cars. I've learned that a cat can't be taught how to cross the road safely. Either a cat knows or he doesn't. This is extremely unfortunate since so many street cats, as well as house cats that explore outside, are hit by cars.

Let me repeat something about the behavior of many drivers in Jerusalem and probably other places that have large populations of street cats. I've often seen drivers slow down and even stop the car if they see a dog in the middle of the road. However, when there's a cat in the road, many drivers ignore it. They continue driving without stopping or slowing down and run over the cat.

Why is that? Who decided that a dog's life is worth more than a cat's? Clearly these are perverted social norms that have no place in any moral code. Morality demands one thing, and people's behavior is something else entirely. At least this is what I've observed of drivers in Jerusalem when they see a cat crossing a road.

Legs held the record when it came to crossing roads. Ever since he learned how to cross safely, he enjoyed going over to the other side of the road and exploring the front gardens there. Often when I returned home by car, I saw him sitting on the stone fence of the house across from outs, looking down from above at the goings-on in the garden.

When Legs reached sexual maturity Nonny made him part of his "warm-up act." Legs remained a member of the community. He slept in other gardens, but he ate and spent a significant amount of time in our yard. Sometimes he explored the nearby gardens for several days. But in the afternoons he always positioned himself on the fence and waited for me. Whenever I returned home, I glanced at the fence along the property across from our house, and if I saw Legs or Gigi there (Gigi's story will be continued later), I felt calm and secure.

One afternoon, when Legs was two and a half years old, he went missing. He wasn't perched on the fence when I got home. I decided to go look for him and find out what was going on. I went outside and immediately saw Legs sitting on the ground next to the fence. When he saw me, he got up and started walking toward me.

I immediately saw that he was walking funny. Given how skilled he was at crossing the road I thought that he couldn't possibly have been hit by a car. I watched his gait closely and saw that he was having a hard time walking. In fact, his whole body seemed to be in pain.

I ran back home and went out into the garden to get a cage. I quickly called the vet and left a message that I was bringing in a sick cat. I returned to the spot where I'd left Legs and he was still there, part lying down and part sitting. I gently put him inside the cage, with his full cooperation, and we drove to the veterinarian.

Legs stayed there for three days. He underwent a thorough examination and extensive tests, but the veterinarian couldn't pin point what was causing such weakness and so quickly too. Legs was diagnosed with a kidney disease, a rather common affliction in cats, but this condition couldn't explain his rapid deterioration. The vet prescribed various drugs and brought Legs back home. I moved him into the huge cage in the pergola and left him there with blankets, newspapers, food, and water.

This is what the veterinarian advised me to do, and I agreed with his assessment, for it was vital to keep an eye on Legs at all times to see if there was any change in his condition. It was also necessary for him to get his medication regularly and on time.

For three days, Legs took all the prescribed drugs but there was no change. I reported back to the veterinarian and we decided that if Legs showed no improvement by the following morning I should take him to the animal hospital where he'd undergo a more thorough battery of tests.

The next morning I woke up with an ominous feeling. I got up and asked myself why I was so sure something awful had happened. My answer was the silence. Each morning Legs was in the huge cage, he woke me up with his cries. There was no doubt that he was in pain and he was waiting for me to provide a painkiller. That morning, there wasn't a sound.

I only took the time to quickly brush my teeth and put on some work clothes, and then I went out to the pergola. It was as I'd feared. Legs lay in the cage, lifeless. His face was calm and he was no longer in pain.

With tears streaming down my face, I closed the cage door. I returned inside, drank some coffee, and showered. I got dressed and called one of my cat-loving friends and asked him to come over so we could bury Legs in nature. And so we did.

Like Tete, Legs too lived a short but very happy life. I keep reminding myself of this fact whenever I am struck by grief over the loss of Tete and Legs. There is some comfort in that. There is also some comfort in knowing that I did everything that could be done to save them.

Unbeknownst to them, cats are Buddhists. They live in the moment. Tete and Legs lived in the present, and though their present didn't last for very long, for them, with their wonderful nature, the present was magnificent and glorious.

Toto: The Cat that Fell from the Sky

One lovely spring day during the time before the pergola existed, I was standing in the garden when a kitten suddenly appeared in midair, as if he had just fallen from the sky. It was a very small kitten, not more than three weeks old. I watched him fall in astonishment and thought he would break his skull. But he was so small and weighed so little that he didn't seem to sustain any injuries. In any case, I quickly came to my senses and approached him. He was lying on the ground, probably in shock from his recent flight, but when I picked him up it was clear that he was fine. He lay like a little chick in my palm. After a few moments, I put him down on the ground and he stood up in the wobbly way kittens his age stand up.

I let him walk around for a bit and explore this new place into which he had fallen. As he was wobbling around, Nonny, a three-month-old kitten at the time, approached the new kitten and started sniffing him.

I left the two of them together and went inside to prepare baby formula, which the kitten clearly needed, and to bring some soft kitten food, which he might be able to eat. When I returned I found Nonny rolling the kitten over and the little one appeared to be enjoying it. I saw that the two kittens were a pair, so right away I made a bed for the newcomer next to Nonny's.

I fed the kitten and put him in his bed, which he had no problem leaving. But it was obvious that he wouldn't be able to get out of the garden. As readers must have realized by now, the fence prevented all kittens from leaving the garden until they were at least a few months old. As I've mentioned before, one section of the fence was significantly lower than the rest, but only larger kittens exit that way. Even mothers wouldn't take their kittens out for their famous border patrols until their kittens were older.

Toto

I named the new kitten Toto. I left the garden as Nonny and Toto each slept in his own bed. When I came out into the garden later to see how Toto was getting along, I was taken aback for a moment when I saw that his bed was empty. I quickly recovered when I looked over at Nonny's bed and saw the two kittens lying close to each other, almost embracing, sleeping soundly. It was such a moving sight. I squatted down and stroked the two of them. They continued sleeping and a sense of security and peace came over me.

The next day I asked myself how Toto could have fallen into my garden. The only logical answer was that the neighbor in the garden next door must have found Toto and without a second thought, picked him up and tossed him over the tall fence separating our two gardens. I was angry with the neighbor who couldn't possibly have known that Toto wouldn't be injured by the fall. The following day, when I saw the neighbor, I asked him if he had thrown a kitten into my garden, and he said that he had. I explained that if Toto had been slightly older, doing this could have ended disastrously. I asked the neighbor to call me in the future if he found another kitten in his garden. He promised to do so, and from that day on, no more kittens came flying into my garden.

As readers already know, because some neighbors saw street cats as a nuisance and occasionally threatened to call the municipal cat catcher, eventually we installed a special fence between our garden and the neighbor's, and we also fenced off the other neighbors' gardens to prevent cats from entering them.

Toto waited for his special meals three times a day. He would finish his portion of baby formula and quickly start to eat the soft kitten food. He and Nonny continued sleeping together. Sometimes they slept in Nonny's bed and sometimes in Toto's.

During the day, Toto played with anything that came his way. He jumped and leaped and twirled around. When he grew tired of playing alone, he found Nonny and start playing with his tail. Nonny played along and moved his tail to and fro, and Toto ran after the twitching tail. When Nonny was preoccupied by his games with the older kittens, Toto tried to join them. The kittens didn't push him away, but he was too little and he naturally ended up playing the role of the ball. Since the kittens didn't hurt him, Toto gladly played his role as a ball on occasion. Sometimes he managed to participate a little in their games and he seemed to be enjoying himself tremendously.

Nonny acted like a mother to Toto. He couldn't fulfill the role of a father, for as we've already seen, a cat's father doesn't really take part in raising it. Even Geezer, who babysat Kitsushi's kittens and taught them a few things, never played a truly significant role in their lives. Nonny was very successful as a mother, which in itself is quite strange since he grew up an orphan and it is not clear to me how he knew what he had to teach Toto.

In any case, Toto's upbringing was exemplary. Nonny taught him leisure activities and various life skills. Toto learned to fight, jump on trees, climb up to the pergola roof and climb down again, and to be assertive when securing food and a house to sleep in. Nonny also taught him manners—namely, how to behave toward kittens, especially those that were weaker than he was, how to conduct himself around females, especially when they were nursing, and how to befriend young males.

Toto was a diligent student and grew into a well-behaved and charming kitten. Unfortunately, Nonny was unforgiving toward Toto once he grew up. When Nonny became the leader, Toto was a sexually mature cat of a significant size. Nonny saw him as a threat to his leadership and started taking steps to drive him away. After about a week during which Nonny made Toto's life a living hell, even though Toto remained passive in the face of Nonny's attacks, Toto got the message.

Tears ran down my cheeks when Toto ate in the yard for the last time. I guessed that he was going to leave us for good because on two previous occasions he had disappeared for two days. He had probably gone searching for an alternative territory. I went over to that beautiful big cat that had arrived as a little fur ball and stroked him for a long time, wishing him a safe journey. The next day there was no trace of him in the garden.

Not a day passed after Toto's departure when I didn't look at other gardens on my way to the supermarket to see whether Toto had found a place there. I couldn't see him. In despair I started getting used to the idea that I would never see Toto again.

As is often the case in these situations, when one consciously gives up on something, it suddenly appears. This is how it happened with Toto. Two months after he left us, I went to the supermarket one morning and saw a beautiful, big, and well-groomed cat crossing the road. There was no doubt in my mind that it was Toto. I waited for him to get out of the road, crossed to his side of the street, and called out his name. He immediately turned his head and ran straight as an arrow toward me. I bent over with boundless joy. Toto was just as happy as I was and wagged his tail as he let me hug him with all my strength. When I was through kissing and hugging him, he accompanied me to the supermarket, right up to the main road.

From that day on, I met Toto at the same time and place several times a month. Unlike other street cats that did not have a place to eat, a place to sleep, and constant care, Toto seemed clean and well groomed. To this day, I still don't know whether he joined another community of cats.

Toto did not appear during mating season and I didn't see him for several weeks. When mating season was over, he reappeared and I continued to meet him and he would accompany me all the way to the road.

After two years, I went out of the house one bitter day and checked to see if Toto was waiting for me across the street. I saw him lying on the side of the road. I ran, possessed, to see what had happened. Toto was lying there, dead, without a drop of blood to be seen. My cat-loving neighbor and I guessed that Toto must have been hit by a car and thrown onto the side of the road. He must have suffered from serious internal bleeding, lost consciousness, and lay there until he died.

I couldn't continue my walk and returned home where I sat down and cried. There is no doubt that Toto died too young. Yet from the moment he was tossed into my garden, his life was a good one and he died a relatively peaceful death.

Chapter 12:
The Pergola Cats:
Turquoise and Pizzo

About a decade ago, five years after the first cat family arrived, we decided to build a pergola in one section of our relatively large garden. Our intention was to improve our quality of life, so we could sit outside in the shade during spring and summer, and remain outside even on cool Jerusalem evenings and nights, which, by the way, are becoming rarer every year.

The pergola was built over two-thirds of the garden and is quite big—bigger than the living room inside our home. Such an addition also opened up new possibilities for entertaining.

The pergola was magnificently built from timber and wooden beams, and its roof was constructed from interconnected plastic boards. Under the roof, in addition to support beams there were also rafters about two feet beneath the roof crisscrossing the length and breadth of the pergola.

We decorated the pergola with suitable plants in large flowerpots, which we bought especially for the pergola from a nursery about an hour and a half away by car (this is a very long drive in Israel). We bought wicker and glass furniture to fit the pergola, and we created a very large sitting area, a spacious dining area, and a laid-back corner with armchairs that turn into beds. We decorated the pergola with cloth and wooden canvases, added various knickknacks for color, and of course installed excellent lighting so we could read comfortably while relaxing in the pergola at night.

We also built the cat pergola next to the one meant for humans, which was rather long and narrow. The cat pergola could be closed in the front and on one side with plastic sheets that could be rolled up and down. In summer we rolled them up to give the cats some air, and in winter we rolled them down to keep out the wind and rain. We put beds with blankets and closed cat houses with beds in the pergola. We also added two low stools and one wicker armchair.

In the remaining L-shaped area, which was about a quarter of the size of the original garden, we had a yard with plants and a small fishpond. In the center was an area covered with gravel where I fed cats in summer, spring, and when the weather was nice in autumn and winter.

The entire area was enclosed by a fence made of stones and topped with green plastic. In one spot that faces the area where both we and our neighbor parked our cars, we left a gap between the stone and the plastic parts so kittens and weak cats could enter the yard. We made sure this opening wasn't facing the road.

We enjoyed our pergola a lot during that first summer. We often sat there, entertained, and even managed to throw a wedding party in the pergola. In short, the pergola really did improve our quality of life. But this paradise, as I've mentioned, lasted for only one summer.

It was autumn and Beauty was raising her kittens, which were still feeding by the front entrance at that time. One day a little white kitten with a single black circle on her body appeared. She had a white and black face and a black tail. She sat alone in the little garden at the entrance to our house. I naturally tried to get close to her, but she ran away the moment she saw me. It was clear that she had lost her mother or that her mother had abandoned her. She was thin and unkempt and far from a pretty sight.

Since Beauty had adopted kittens before and raised them with her own, I hoped that she would do so again. And she did. A few days later, I saw the white kitten lying next to Beauty. The other kittens also learned to accept her and she was officially adopted. The kitten's eyes were turquoise, so that's what I named her , though I often called her by two nicknames, Turqi and Tushi.

Turqi began "taking shape" and her life underwent a radical change. She was no longer lonely. She had a mother, and she had brothers and sisters. Anyone looking in on her life from the outside could not have guessed that she had been adopted, except for her unusual color.

This was a successful litter and all four of Beauty's kittens developed well. Fortunately, even after they stopped nursing, they didn't get sick, though they were still too young to be vaccinated. As readers already know, this is the most dangerous time in a kitten's life.

Turquoise (Turqi)

I was happy for the healthy and active family, which had already started coming into the yard, when one morning I saw that only Turqi remained out front after the others had gone. I went over to her, and though she hardly ever let me touch her before, which is typical for females, this time she let me stroke her and I could feel how thin she was. I looked at her carefully and saw that she didn't seem well. The next day it was obvious that Turqi was sick. The main symptom was constant diarrhea.

The veterinarian prescribed antibiotic tablets and instructed me to feed her only a special type of food. I did as he said and Turqi's condition improved. She seemed to be recuperating. But after the diarrhea had stopped for two weeks, it reappeared. It wasn't hard to figure out that once Turqi started feeling better, she jumped into the yard, ate regular cat food, and got sick again.

I sat and thought about the situation but I couldn't come up with any other solution except to bring Turqi inside the house or the human pergola to ensure that she couldn't get into the yard. This was the only way to prevent her from getting sick again.

I tried to bring Turqi indoors, but she didn't do well in enclosed spaces and would often run amok and jump on the walls. After a few unsuccessful days, I transferred her to the human pergola. There, in the spacious pergola, Turqi felt fine. It goes without saying that she ate only her special healthy food while there. Out of concern that she'd manage to eat the regular cat food in the yard if I let her out, I decided to leave her in the pergola for the time being.

Little Turqi chewed and scratched anything she could get her teeth into or paws on, and little by little the pergola was destroyed. I brought two cat beds into the pergola and put one in a warm spot and the other in a cooler spot so Turqi could choose which she preferred and hopefully stop sleeping in the flower pots. Of course I also added a litter box. Since Turqi couldn't be allowed to eat regular food, I bought special containers for the regular cat food, which I began storing in the pergola. In short, the pergola quickly became Turqi's home and a pantry for the other street cats' food.

Little by little, it dawned on me that I had in fact given up the pergola and all its comforts. At first, I thought that we would be able to continue using the pergola ourselves and to entertain our guests there. So many people keep cats at home, so one cat in the pergola shouldn't be a problem. Yet I quickly saw that this was impossible. Turqi never became a domesticated cat and remained a wild street cat in every way.

I'll never forget my one and only attempt at having my friends over for lunch in the pergola after Turqi had lived there for a while. I set the table properly and went back inside to get some more things. When I came back out again, the tablecloth and everything that had been on it were on the floor, and Turqi was dancing among the dishes and pulling at the tablecloth with all her strength. Turqi was convinced of my great love for her, and rightly so. She probably knew deep down that she wouldn't be punished for her bad behavior.

I somehow managed to get through lunch by keeping a constant eye on Turqi and sending my guests inside with instructions about what to bring out. Although we ate in the sitting area, Turqi wasn't at all shy, and in full view of everyone she constantly tried to jump on the wicker and glass table and grab anything she could. I was fortunate that my guests were all animal lovers, but even they understood right away and told me that they thought it would be impossible to have guests in the pergola when Turqi was around.

After that, I stopped entertaining friends in the pergola, but I kept sitting there, reading, listening to music, and enjoying the outdoors.

But the havoc that Turqi wreaked in the pergola that winter made it unpleasant for me to sit there, to put it mildly. This is how Turqi came to have a huge house all to herself, where she could do whatever she pleased.

Spaying Turqi didn't calm her down, either, and I started limiting my time in the pergola to playtime with Turqi or to prepare food for the cats in the yard.

Turqi, who was only growing larger while living outside, would sometimes try to escape the pergola. Since she was a particularly clever and crafty cat, her escapes were always meticulously planned. She studied my habits and the first time she escaped—about a year after she moved into the pergola—she waited for me to open the door to the yard with my hands full of cat food, and before I could manage to shut the door behind me, she flew out—yes, she almost flew.

As usual, I became anxious. I quickly fed the cats, returned home, and went outside again to look for Turqi. The moment I stepped outside I saw her sitting calmly in our parking space. I went over to her and called her name, certain that she would be happy to see me and return home. I was gravely mistaken. The moment she saw me she sprinted away from the parking space, ran across the street, and disappeared into one of the gardens.

I continued running and searching for her, constantly calling her name. There is no doubt that anxious people forget all logic. In any case, my search failed. I returned home, prepared a cup of coffee, and began to think. It occurred to me that the next time I fed the cats, Turqi might be there with them.

This was indeed what happened. I went out with cat food and out of the corner of my eye I saw Turqi standing at the edge of the garden, looking at me. I left the pergola door ajar so she could get in if she wanted to, and lo and behold, after I moved just a few steps away from the door, Turqi leaped from her spot and ran inside the pergola through the opening that I had left. I hurried to close the door behind her, feeling deliriously happy. That year, Turqi managed to escape from the pergola two more times and returned the same way as she did the first time.

It was a lovely spring day when Turqi managed to escape for the fourth time. This time she didn't show up with the rest of the cats at mealtime, so of course I walked from yard to yard calling her name in vain. It occurred to me that this time she might be afraid of the cats in the yard, most of which she didn't know, and that she might try to return through the front door, since she knew this part of the house from her kittenhood. I felt weighed down with worry.

I opened the door every half hour or so and the third time I was happy to see Turqi sitting comfortably on the stairs. The moment the door opened and I moved out of the way she leaped inside, and I closed the door after her. She explored the house, as she typically did, and then stood near the door to the pergola and asked to be let out. Over the years she escaped three more times, and this was her way of coming back home.

It wouldn't be an overstatement to say that I lived in constant fear that Turqi might manage to escape again. Who knew if she'd decide to return?

Turqi had a nightly habit of standing on the windowsill inside the pergola, which faces the living room. That's where she stood and waited for me to come to the window. The moment I arrived, she jumped off the windowsill and ran to her bed near the door to the living room and waited for me there. Like an indentured servant, I walk to the pergola door, where I had to kneel down and put "the lady" to bed while repeatedly saying, "Good Turqi, good girl." This process could last for ten minutes and repeat itself several times per evening. Since Turqi's needs were a high priority for me, I would usually humor her and tuck her into bed again and again. I have no doubt that I raised a neurotic cat. There's a reason people say that pets come to resemble their owner's character.

For four years, Turqi lived and reigned over the pergola alone. And then her solitary existence came to an end. It was a harsh Jerusalem winter. Sophie had disappeared somewhere to give birth to her kittens. She appeared for all meals but quickly vanished afterward. One particularly rainy day I went out to feed the cats in their pergola, when suddenly I heard meowing distinctly coming from the basement, which was located, as I've mentioned, at one end of the cat pergola. I went over to the basement and saw that the door was indeed slightly open; a cat had clearly entered the basement and brought her kittens inside. Since Sophie was the only female in the community that brought her kittens into the basement, I concluded in a veritable Sherlock Holmes feat of reasoning that the meowing kittens belonged to Sophie.

I looked around and saw that Sophie was standing nearby, eating leisurely. I had no choice but to open the basement door and take a look. I expected to find at least four kittens, but instead I saw a solitary kitten that at first glance looked like a white chick.

I gently picked up the kitten—it was a female—and together we left the basement. In the light, the kitten was the spitting image of her mother: white with lines of gray and ginger brown, which looked like painted watercolors. I brought the kitten over to Sophie. She was indeed hers. Sophie cleaned the kitten and even lay on one of the beds and nursed her, but only for a few minutes. Soon afterward Sophie gave me a long look that seemed to say, "She's all yours," and she promptly jumped out of the garden.

It was clear that for some reason Sophie couldn't or wouldn't raise the kitten. Either she had run out of milk or she had other kittens somewhere else. In any case, she entrusted this kitten to me.

Naturally, I couldn't just leave the kitten in the cat pergola or in Turqi's pergola because she was so small that she could have easily gotten lost. I thought about what to do next. The most humane option seemed to be to bring her into the house. However, from my experience with Sophie and her kittens I knew that kittens, however small, would not tolerate being indoors. The second option was to put a bed with warm blankets in the basement, put some special kitten food and water nearby, and leave her in that familiar environment.

The first thing I did after repeatedly petting the kitten and calming her down was to put her on the ground. Then I arranged the basement to be a comfortable and pleasant temporary home. After I saw the kitten wobbling toward the bed in her touching and funny way and nibbling the soft kitten food on her way there, I calmed down and left the basement.

For the next three weeks I went down into the basement three times a day, cleaned, tidied up, and took the kitten outside. By then I'd christened her Pizzo. I sat with her in the open air for at least half an hour each time, letting her skip around and run to and fro. Afterward I returned her to the basement. The absence of any mewing from the basement indicated that Pizzo was content with the situation, meaning she wasn't hungry, or cold, or bored. Since I could hear everything that went on in the basement from the living room, I was sure that Pizzo was safe.

After three weeks, when I took her out for a walk, I looked at her closely and thought that she was now too big to disappear into some hole. I brought her into Turqi's pergola, put her down on the floor, and waited to see how she would be received.

To my astonishment, the moment Pizzo saw Turqi, she immediately ran over to her. After sniffing Pizzo for a few minutes, Turqi started licking her with purpose. Pizzo's life in the basement ended and her life in the pergola with Turqi began.

Turqi accepted Pizzo as if she were her own kitten. Her instincts told her how to be a mother and she behaved toward Pizzo exactly as mothers do toward their kittens: she groomed her, played with her, and taught her all the wonders of the pergola and all the secrets of life, as she knew them.

When Pizzo was small, she and Turqi slept in the same bed. When winter was over and spring arrived, I placed two beds next to each other, but Pizzo often crept into Turqi's bed and lay on her.

I sometimes wondered at Turqi's dramatic transformation. Her experience of partial motherhood helped her mature. She no longer tried to run away, nor did she stand on the windowsill every evening waiting for me to tuck her in. It was a pleasure to watch Turqi let Pizzo eat first and only later approach her plate. Of course, from the moment Pizzo arrived, Turqi was exposed to regular cat food. She certainly shared the food that I gave Pizzo, but she never got sick. I concluded that her digestive system issue had resolved itself.

Pizzo

I planned to have Pizzo spayed when she was seven months old, but for some reason I forgot all about it. One evening when Pizzo was around that age, I returned home and was greeted by heart-wrenching cries coming from the pergola. I ran to see what was happening and saw Pizzo running around like a mad cat, her back completely arched, making fierce sounds that I interpreted as cries of pain.

I immediately called the veterinarian and explained in a deluge of words that something terrible must have happened to the cat that I had an appointment to be spayed. I explained that something serious had happened and that she must have injured her back. To his credit, the veterinarian didn't burst out laughing at my outburst. He waited for me to finish describing the situation and then quietly told me, "Raphaella, Pizzo is simply in heat. Her arched back is a typical characteristic of a female in heat preparing to mate, and the cries are her way of letting males know that she is waiting for them." I immediately calmed down and wasn't at all ashamed that I had misunderstood the situation. In all my years of experience with street cats, I had never seen a cat in such a state.

I went through another incident with Pizzo when she was young. Like many cat owners, I sometimes bought or received toys for kittens to play with. Although I'm quite suspicious of most toys, as I've already explained, for some reason I bought Pizzo a long stick with a woolen mouse tied to one end and a long elastic string tied to the other. I used to tie the elastic string somewhere high and Pizzo would jump, catch the mouse, and pull on it with all her strength. The moment she let go, the string would snap back, pulling the stick and mouse. I had no experience with such complicated toys, but I didn't foresee any problem. After all, what could possibly happen? It turned out that quite a lot could go wrong.

One evening when I returned home, I was once again greeted with terrible cries, which I immediately identified as Pizzo's. Again, I ran to the pergola and this time discovered that Pizzo was in trouble. She must have really pulled hard on the mouse. The elastic string had snapped loose and Pizzo continued playing with the toy on the ground. The string was tangled around her front legs in such a way that every effort she made to free herself only further tightened the string and caused her pain.

I went over to her and tried to calm her down and untangle the string from her legs, but without success. She was in such a state of panic that she wouldn't let me come near her. I almost despaired and was about to call my cat-loving friend to help me free Pizzo. I decided to give it one more try. I somehow managed to coax Pizzo inside the house with the string wrapped around her legs. I picked up a pair of special scissors, which wouldn't injure Pizzo, and with great cunning I stroked her head with one hand and with the other tried to cut the string in the middle. I succeeded on the second try. Finally the string could no longer hurt her since now half was wrapped around one leg and half around the other.

It was time to take the string off her legs. I brought her delicious sardines and while she ate them, I managed to cut the string off one leg. Other delicacies were necessary to get the string off the other leg. When the entire procedure was over, Pizzo ran back to the pergola as if nothing had happened and started playing with Turqi, who had stood there watching the entire time I was taking care of Pizzo.

Needless to say, I quickly threw the toy away, and I also made a point of calling the pet store and warning them about how dangerous it could be. When I went to the store a week later, I was happy to see that there was no trace of this toy for sale or of any other toy attached to an elastic string.

Pizzo was a fantastic climber and her behavior in the pergola reminded me of monkeys. She particularly liked to climb up the large supporting rafters about a foot beneath the plastic boards that form the roof of the pergola. I was always impressed by Pizzo's ability to jump and the way she would lay, even sleep, on a rafter without any fear of heights.

One day, when I went to put out some food, only Turqi approached the plate. Pizzo was nowhere to be seen. I instinctively looked up but couldn't see her. I assumed that she was sleeping in some flowerpot or hiding in some corner. But it was quite rare for Pizzo to be absent at mealtime. So when the same thing happened the next day, after she came as usual for breakfast but missed lunch, I began to think that she might not be feeling well. I looked for her all over the pergola but couldn't find her. I checked the pergola doors, but they were securely locked. I didn't understand what was happening. Only when I saw Pizzo again during dinner did I calm down.

I kept trying to figure out where Pizzo had gone on those two occasions. The mystery was solved by the young woman who cleaned our house. She came and told me that she had seen Pizzo pushing apart two plastic boards in the roof, creating a hole through which she stuck her head. We went out to the pergola and the young woman showed me where Pizzo had managed to do this. I looked closely and saw that there was a handsome gap between two of the roof's plastic boards, near where the roof connected to the cat pergola. I returned inside and stood in the living room, watching Pizzo's activities through the window.

Indeed, the moment I left, Pizzo quickly climbed up to the scene of the crime, exited through the gap she had created, and stood on the roof of the pergola.

I was concerned that Pizzo would try to climb down from the pergola to the yard. And since she had never been in the yard or outside, she wouldn't know how to return. I was glad to see that she was only leaping around the roof without trying to get down.

It was clear that the situation needed to be handled quickly. I called the pergola contractor and explained the situation. Luckily he was fond of cats and made time that very day to come over and fix the gap between the plastic boards. He also inspected the other boards and made sure that there weren't any additional gaps. Of course, all this had to happen while Pizzo was in the pergola, not on the roof. So I made sure that Pizzo remained inside by staying in the pergola with her for over two hours, until the contractor arrived. In my presence, Pizzo didn't dare pull her little trick.

Since that day, Pizzo managed to push apart boards in different locations twice, and the whole story repeated itself. I never knew what to expect.

If readers are wondering why Turqi didn't take advantage of the gap that Pizzo created and sneak outside to the roof, the answer is simple: Turqi was just too big and fat to fit through the opening, which was barely large enough for the significantly skinnier Pizzo.

Turqi and Pizzo got along well, sometimes very well. One of the few reasons they fought was over their preferred bed. For some reason one bed always seemed better than the other to them, come rain or shine, and the cat that got this bed was the winner. I tried to ensure that both beds were equal. Not only were the beds themselves identical, but the blankets and other rags, which cats love, were also the same in both beds. Any yet they always perceived one bed, and it was always a different bed, to be markedly superior.

After Pizzo grew up, Turqi resumed her custom of standing on the windowsill, waiting for me to tuck her in. Sometimes when this happened in the middle of a good movie I ground my teeth but always went to Turqi. A movie just couldn't compare to my love for this cat.

Despite Turqi and my close relationship, she only ever let me pet her sparingly. She just didn't like a human to touch her fur. Pizzo let me pet her more, but she too could suddenly jump on me and pretend to scratch me. I say "pretend" because her claws were always retracted, so I usually was not really scratched.

Turqi came inside the house from time to time to explore and she certainly knew the house and could find her way out. Pizzo, on the other hand, did enter the house from time to time, but the moment she got inside, she seemed to panic and very quickly began to look for a way out. I always had to help her find the door to the pergola. Both of them certainly remained untamed street cats.

Readers probably realize that ever since Pizzo joined Turqi in the pergola, the amount of damage only increased. It went from a pergola for humans to Turqi and Pizzo's pergola. It might sound crazy, but it's true that I let it happen. But I don't see how I could have reacted any differently given the circumstances, and I am sure that if faced with a similar situation again today I would make the same decisions again.

I console myself by thinking that we probably wouldn't have continued using the pergola because of mosquitos and other nuisances. In addition, Turqi and Pizzo's presence in the pergola prevented mice from entering the house from the basement. There was a mouse problem in my neighborhood, especially when construction was happening and the ground was dug up. So at least we were spared this problem by the cat pergola.

However, I don't delude myself that this was the reason I accepted the loss of the pergola. The real reason is that one probably has to be a little crazy to take care of twenty street cats, and this drama with the pergola was just part of the madness.

Chapter 13: The Pergola Infiltrators: Cloud and Red

The pergola was indeed home to Turqi (also known as Tushi) and Pizzo, but it was infiltrated twice by young female kittens. This is their story. When Sophie, Pizzo's mother, gave birth to one last litter, there was one odd-looking kitten. She had a black fur, but underneath it, her coat was white. The white fur wasn't quite visible, probably because of the black fur. Since she was an odd and undefined color, I called her Cloud. Sophie stayed with her last litter for three months and then stopped paying attention to the kittens.

Cloud

The Pergola Infiltrators: Cloud and Red

Autumn arrived and the nights became chillier. Then one evening, as I was looking out at the pergola, I suddenly got the feeling that there was another cat besides Turqi and Pizzo, who were in their beds. I thought I was imagining things, or beings, because how could another cat get into the pergola? I was sure that when I opened and closed the pergola that day I hadn't seen a cat sneaking in. Of course there was an occasional infiltration when a cat quickly darted in through the pergola door as I came out with food. After a few minutes inside, the infiltrators always wanted to leave and started jumping around the pergola as if possessed. I had to call for help to get them out. One person would stand near the open door to make sure that no other cats came in, while someone else would show the infiltrator the way out by calling to the cat and clapping. This process could take up to ten minutes, but eventually to the infiltrator's great relief we would rescue it from the pergola. This time, however, I was sure that no cat had gotten in. I went over to the beds. In summer, spring, and autumn the beds were located at the other end of the pergola from the door to the living room. As I came closer, I saw that we did in fact have a visitor. Cloud was lying in one bed while Turqi and Pizzo were walking around the pergola. When I came even closer, she spooked, jumped off the bed, and hid behind one of the flowerpots. I decided that the right thing to do was to let her be and I left the pergola.

I returned inside the house. I admit I was curious and impatient to find out how Cloud had entered the pergola. When I went outside again to give the cats their next meal, there was Cloud in the yard with all the other cats. The kitten had left the pergola and returned to the yard.

I realized that Cloud had found a way to enter and exit the pergola and there was nothing to do but accept this fact and find out how she did it to satisfy my curiosity. It took me several days to discover that

Cloud had found a spot where a gap between the pergola's wooden beams was a little wider than usual. Since she was small and thin, she had no problem wriggling her way through the gap. Cloud adopted a lifestyle that allowed her to enjoy both worlds. On one hand, she had the warmth and security of the pergola and constant access to food, and on the other hand, she didn't have to give up the yard with all its attractions, or her explorations of other gardens.

Given their size, Turqi or even Pizzo couldn't have used the narrow gap and I decided to leave it open and allow Cloud to enjoy herself without worrying about the other two cats. And so for a few months Cloud lived in the pergola and outside, and when winter came, she spent most of her time in the pergola. Luckily for her, she was a small kitten, and it's possible she even dieted to maintain her slim figure—in any case, even though she grew and developed during those months, she still managed to fit through the gap.

I tried to catch her and have her spayed, but I was unsuccessful. I thought that when she reached sexual maturity, she would venture outside and it would remain to be seen whether she'd return to the pergola. It was clear that if she got pregnant she would no longer be able to pass through the gap, but all that was still in the future.

In the meantime, an interesting thing happened in the pergola. The day after Cloud moved into the pergola, Pizzo adopted her as if she were her own daughter. They slept in the same bed and Pizzo licked her all over, played with her, and performed all a mother's duties toward a three-month-old kitten. Cloud seemed to enjoy it immensely, perhaps because she was a small kitten and no longer had a mother since Sophie, as usual, had left her kittens relatively early.

Turqi was left alone but she didn't seem to mind. She lay down or sat up and looked at Pizzo and Cloud enjoying their various activities together. Only rarely did Turqi join the two or respond to Cloud's invitation to spend some quality time with her.

Spring was at the door, the season of transition, and Cloud still wasn't in heat. During the winter, Cloud hadn't tried to leave the pergola even once, but she ate like there was no tomorrow and grew bigger and fatter. It was clear that she could no longer come and go through the gap between the wooden beams, and I waited for her to decide where she wanted to live her life—in the pergola or outside. When spring finally arrived, Cloud became restless and the expected happened. One morning when I went out to feed the cats, Cloud quickly jumped past me and ran out of the pergola.

For two months, Cloud continued to live in the yard and appear for all meals. On a few occasions, she even managed to jump back into the pergola when I opened the door, and she would stay in there for a day or two. Whenever Cloud returned, her close relationship with Pizzo resumed as if she'd never left.

Spring passed and summer arrived, and it's possible that Cloud finally came into heat. She was still living in the garden but began missing meals for several days in row. She didn't seem pregnant to me, but she no longer tried to jump back into the pergola. Then, one summer day, she arrived for a meal, ate, jumped out of the garden, and was never seen again.

To this day when I walk through the neighborhood, I look around searching for Cloud. Her appearance was so distinctive that I am sure I would notice her. Unfortunately I still haven't seen her. As a female, if she found another place to live, there is no chance that she would return to visit her home and Pizzo.

A similar story happened just six months ago. One of the cats that had arrived in the garden from who knows where and that had become a member of the community gave birth in the garden to a very unsuccessful litter. The kittens were premature and didn't survive, except for one kitten that managed to beat the odds. Like Cloud, she too had an oddly colored coat. She appeared to be a tabby, but this Stripy had ginger red dots and her whole appearance was reddish. I naturally called her Red; I even mentioned her briefly in Chapter 7.

Red

Red grew up alone. Her mother did nurse her for six weeks, but the kitten started eating with the adult cats before she stopped nursing. She was born in the middle of winter and found shelter from the rain and wind inside one for the houses in the cat pergola. Unfortunately many cats are scared of entering a closed cat house, so during the harshest days of winter they leave the cat pergola and find shelter under houses, in the corners of stairwells, and in other hiding places known only to them.

Red was not afraid of a closed cat house and when I saw that she lived inside one, I made sure to change the newspapers and blanket every time it rained, and I placed the house very close to the pergola. This is how Red spent most of our short winter.

Toward the end of winter, when she was still small and skinny, Red discovered the gap through which Cloud had entered the pergola followed in her footsteps. Turqi and Pizzo were in their winter beds near the living room door, and the autumn, summer, and spring beds were at the other end of the pergola. Red got into one of them and spent the few remaining cold days of the season there. Like Cloud, Red also came and went as she pleased.

I am sad to say that unlike with Cloud, no bond formed between Red and Pizzo or Turqi, though they did her no harm and tolerated her presence. They also let her share their food, but she almost always preferred to go outside and eat with the other cats.

Red's life in the pergola was short. She went into heat at a very young age when she was still quite small, and so she left the pergola. I called a special cat catcher to try to trap her because it was obvious to all who saw her that she was too small to handle pregnancy and giving birth. If she were to get pregnant, the result would clearly be tragic. The kittens probably wouldn't survive, and her life might also be in danger.

The cat catcher appeared as scheduled at seven in the morning and placed his special cage in the garden with a tuna delicacy inside it. Red was the first to enter the cage, but there was a technical problem and the string that the catcher was supposed to pull to trap the cat inside the cage didn't work for some reason. Red simply ate the tuna at her leisure and then walked back out of the cage. The cat catcher tried to interest her in the cage again, but in vain. Eventually she jumped over the fence and left the garden.

And so it happened that Red got pregnant when she was much too young and small. During the first couple of weeks, she still managed to squeeze her body through the gap between the beams and spent a few nights and days in the pergola. But soon she had grown too big and couldn't enter the pergola, or didn't want to.

I didn't see her first litter because the kittens must have been stillborn. The second litter came shortly after the first, before Red could recover from having given birth at such a young age. This litter was also problematic and only one ginger kitten survived; its story will be told later.

As I've already mentioned, nature sometimes makes mistakes and a female kitten comes into heat before her time, or before she has fully developed. When this happens to street cats that are not cared for as mine are, the pregnancy usually ends in disaster. Like Red, a similarly untimely pregnancy occurred to another cat in my community, but fortunately, after this female had her first litter of stillborn kittens, she didn't come into heat again until she had grown sufficiently.

Even after Red gave birth, she no longer tried to enter the pergola, and for over six months she didn't get pregnant. She lived a happy life during those months and her best friend was the spayed Tricolor. But her life with me ended just as Cloud's had. Red began to disappear, even though she barely knew the territory due to having spent most of her life in the garden. At first she disappeared for a day or two, and what happened afterward should be clear to readers by now. One day she ate her breakfast, left, and never returned.

It's interesting that I missed Red as much as I missed Cloud. I searched for her around the neighborhood and I still keep an eye out for her whenever I'm out outside.

The two pergola infiltrators that left me were smart, cunning cats, and first-class survivors. These are the qualities that enabled them to find a way into the pergola and enjoy the best of both worlds. Though I have no idea if this is significant, the interesting thing is that both of them had extremely unusual coats, the likes of which I haven't seen since.

Chapter 14: Cats by Coat Color

These days most of my street cats are tabbies. Most have a uniform coat, but some cats have white patches, usually around the stomach and legs. A few are Furries, but most cats have ordinary short fur. I also have one black and white cat that comes and goes, three tricolor cats (white, black, and ginger), two black cats, one ginger cat, and one gray cat.

Over the years, the dominant colors in the community changed. At first most members of the community had coats similar to the first family: gray, gray and white, and tabbies. Over time and with new cats from elsewhere joining the community, changes began to occur that continue to this day.

Is there a link between coat color and a cat's personality? I have only partial answers to this question. In this chapter I will tell stories of tricolor females, ginger males, and black and white cats, as all the stories told so far did not include cats with coats of these colors.

Tricolor Females and Ginger Males

It all began with a female cat that lived and ate in the garden across the street that belonged to neighbor. The cat's name was Tricolor after her coat, which contained patches of white, ginger, and black. During the first two years of observing my cat community, I only saw Tricolor when I walked around the neighborhood. She never came into my garden. However, life is full of changes and surprises. One day I found Tricolor in my garden, lying comfortably in the sun, undisturbed by the rest of the cats. From that day forward she began appearing in the garden from time to time, but she still didn't eat with the other cats. After she got used to the area, the smell of the wet cat food that I mixed with the dry food piqued her interest, and she began joining us for meals. At first her visits were sporadic, but over time, she began to eat all her meals in my garden while continuing to live in my neighbor's garden.

Tricolor

When mating season arrived, Tricolor got pregnant. She gave birth to her first litter in the garden across the street, but when the kittens were about one month old, she brought them to me. The kittens introduced color into the garden. Two were ginger males, one female was a tricolor, and only one kitten, another female, was a tabby. The ginger cats had different coat patterns. One looked like a panther, which is how he got his name. The other resembled a tiger, and so we called him Tiger. The coat of the tricolor kitten was a bit more faded than her mother's, but three colors were clearly present, so I called her Three.

Tricolor was a good mother and stayed with her kittens for four months. Like the cat pergola mothers, she not only fulfilled the necessary functions of a mother, like grooming and nursing the kittens, but she also taught them to defend themselves and to attack, as well as to climb up to the roof of the pergola and get down by using either the wooden beams or the nearby tree. She even played with the kittens for hours on end, and when they played with her tail, she seemed to enjoy it just as much as they did. She also taught them mealtime manners. Her kittens knew that they had to wait until their mother found herself a plate; only then could they run and find their own plates. However, if one of the kittens failed to find a place among the feeding cats, Tricolor would leave her meal and bring the kitten over to her own plate and let it eat the remainder of the food.

The relationship between Tricolor and her family and the community cats was never a warm one. They simply lived side by side. There were never any fights, but there also weren't any hugs and kisses. I believe that if Tricolor had gotten in trouble and couldn't care for her kittens, the other mothers in the community would not have come to her aid. To them she remained a stranger.

Nevertheless, it seemed that Tricolor was content with the situation. She was certainly a highly individualistic and suspicious cat. She never let me pet her and every time the cat catcher arrived to trap cats to be neutered or spayed, she managed to evade him. She simply didn't enter the cage.

She eventually had a second and then a third litter. When the kittens were one month old and could eat soft food by themselves, Tricolor once again moved them from their birthplace into my garden. This was the pattern she followed with every litter: Tricolor occupied one corner of the garden with her kittens, completely separate from the females and kittens in the community. Her kittens became independent at a relatively young age, and most of them left the garden for good when they reached sexual maturity (I will tell of the three that remained later).

Tricolor was the kind of mother that didn't take her kittens to a distant garden and leave them there once she decided that they were grown-up and could fend for themselves. Instead, she was the one to leave my garden, and the kittens stayed. She returned once she had given birth again, by which time the kittens from her previous litter were almost sexually mature and she must have assumed that they had forgotten her.

I was very curious to see if the kittens had indeed forgotten her, so I carefully observed the initial reactions of the grown-up kittens to their mother's return. In my opinion, the kittens remembered her. Some even tried to approach her and her new kittens. In two cases, she encouraged their attention and allowed Three, for example, to help her babysit the new kittens. But toward most of the kittens from her previous litter, she displayed complete indifference and they gave up trying to get close to her and went back to life as usual.

Over the years that Tricolor brought her kittens to me and raised them in my garden or yard, I became familiar with her personality. Even though she never let me pet her, over time she learned to show her appreciation toward me for taking care of her, and especially for taking care of her kittens. When I administered antibiotics to one or more kittens, she would sit quietly next to me and wait for me to finish the treatment. Afterward she would rub up against my legs for quite some time. She also greeted me when I came out into the garden by moving her tail about in a very interesting pattern, which I believe indicated happiness. I felt that with the passage of time, she and I became good friends and enjoyed a relationship of mutual trust and deep affection.

I was sure that Tricolor would stay with us for the rest of her life, but she had other plans. When she finished raising the third litter she brought to me, she disappeared. Although she always moved back into my neighbor's garden once she decided that her kittens could fend for themselves, this time was different. I didn't see her anywhere outside. When I asked my neighbor where she was, she told me that she thought that Tricolor was living in my garden, whereas I thought that Tricolor was with her. We both found it surprising that for years Tricolor had lived either in my neighbor's garden or in mine.

Two weeks after her disappearance, Tricolor returned to the yard. She was thinner, hungry, and tired, but she certainly looked pleased with herself. She ate and slept well for a few days, wagged her tail at me, rubbed up against me, and behaved as usual. Sometimes she jumped on the fence, crossed the road, and spent a few hours in my neighbor's garden.

One morning, Tricolor disappeared again. A phone call to my neighbor revealed that she wasn't at her place either. We hoped that she would return from her adventure once more, but Tricolor did not come back. She has been gone ever since.

Six months after she vanished, I thought I saw her on the roof of a small house in our neighborhood in a completely different cat territory. She was too far away for me to know for sure if it was she. Her movements were just like Tricolor's. She sat on the roof and surveyed the world, looking quite happy and content. Who knows? It might very well have been Tricolor.

Why did Tricolor disappear? This touches on a topic I've mentioned a few times concerning the disappearance of healthy female cats once they have given birth a few times and have reached the age of five or six. It is clear why males that have reached sexual maturity leave the community—they are either driven away by the leader after they try to challenge him unsuccessfully, or they choose to avoid the confrontation and leave of their own free will. They seek out a new territory for themselves without a leader, or with an old and weak leader that can be challenged. If they fail to gain leadership in another territory, they are doomed to roam from yard to yard, remaining in one place only until a more powerful male drives them out. But why a female in her prime chooses to leave the community of her own free will something I can't explain.

Since females that leave are usually cats that didn't fit in with the community and remained strangers like Sophie and Tricolor, one explanation, perhaps the most plausible, is that they were lonely and tried to find a friendlier environment in another territory. Fitting into a community is usually a problem for new cats from outside looking to join, but even some cats born to females in the community cannot fit in.

Another explanation, which doesn't exclude the first one, is that males in the territory are not to the female's liking. In Sophie's case, she left after two unsuccessful litters and this might have disqualified the community's males in her eyes. After all, for animals the purpose of mating is the preservation and increase of the species (some say it's a dominant factor for humans too). If a female's litters are unsuccessful, it's time to look for new mates.

The second explanation didn't apply to Tricolor since her litters were always successful. Perhaps she just grew tired of the cats in the community, which she didn't particularly like.

The other tricolor female that I want to talk about is Tricolor's daughter from the first litter that she brought over, Three. Despite her two ginger brothers, Three grew up practically alone. The brothers were very close and they tried to include Three in their activities, but she chose to be like her mother, an individualist. Sometimes she played with her brothers but for the first few months of her life she spent most of her time with her mother. When Tricolor left her kittens so they could become independent, Three was mentally and physically prepared for the transition. She used to climb up onto the roof of the pergola very quickly, using the tree rather than the pergola beams. She spent hours on the roof, dancing and having fun in the large space, which she always visited when it was empty. I often watched her from our second floor balcony, feeling content when I saw Three's "independence jig." If other cats climbed onto the roof of the pergola, Three would quickly climb down and disappear into one of the corners of the garden, or jump outside to explore the neighboring gardens.

Three

She got pregnant relatively late when she was eleven months old. She gave birth to her kittens in some unknown location and arrived in my garden with just two kittens in tow. One was white and gray and the other was a ginger cat with white feet, a white stomach, and a white patch on the tip of his tail.

It was immediately obvious that the kittens had different fathers. The white and gray kitten was bigger than a regular kitten and the ginger and white one was ordinary in size. The kittens grew up close to each other and their mother. Three was an incredibly devoted mother. Perhaps she was such a good mother because Tricolor let her help raise her younger brothers and sisters that were part of Tricolor's second litter.

For three months, life for this new family was pleasant, warm, and happy. The kittens, which I named Doll and Gigi, developed well and were accomplished in the many educational games that they played with their mother.

Gradually I began to notice that Three was playing less and less with her kittens. Instead, she was lying for increasing long periods of time in her preferred armchair. She still groomed her kittens and from time to time got off the armchair to eat and use the litter box, but there were no more games. I also noticed that she stopped making the special, unique sounds she used to call her kittens to her.

It took me a while to realize that she was sick. Since she wouldn't let me put her in a cage, I called the veterinarian and asked him to make a house call. To my astonishment, Three let me hold her while the vet listened to her heart and lungs. When the examination was over, the veterinarian told me that he thought that Three was suffering from acute laryngitis (an inflammation that causes a narrowing of the throat) and a weak heart. He prescribed some medicines and said that there was a chance she would recover from the laryngitis, but he wasn't sure about her heart.

With Three's wholehearted cooperation, we began the treatment process. Only a small number of cats ever cooperated with me in this way. The result was that the laryngitis gradually improved and Three began meowing again, though more softly. Her kittens once again slept with her in the armchair, and Three began taking longer walks around the garden. However, with time it became clear that Three's heart condition would remain.

Doll

During all that time, right up until they were eight months old, Doll and Gigi protected and cared for their mother. It almost seemed like their roles were reversed and they became her parents. Doll grew up very quickly and was a large cat even at the age of five months. He would save his mother a place at his plate of food and drive away any cat that tried to sit in her wicker armchair. Gigi kept his mother company for several hours a day. He would play in front of her, bring her various insects that he had caught, and sometimes he would bring her a visitor: Nonny the leader, who at that time was just starting his reign. Three would lie down with her eyes open and enjoy the sights around her; she enjoyed looking at nature and seeing her kittens grow up.

When mating season arrived, Three did not go into heat. As anyone who cares for cats knows, this is typical for a sick cat. It's nature's way of protecting her from the exhausting process of mating, pregnancy, and birth.

Doll was soon driven away by Nonny, who realized that within a few months Doll would be able to beat him in a fight for leadership. As a result, Nonny attacked Doll while he still could. After the fight, which Nonny just barely managed to win, Doll left the garden for good. Given his size, I'm sure he found a territory where he beat the leader and took his place as the dominant male. It's possible that he did this in several territories since he was an avid traveler. Ever since he was five months old, he began disappearing from the garden on long trips through the neighborhood.

Unlike Doll, Gigi was of average size. Ever since Three got sick, Gigi and Nonny had been close. Nonny was kind to him and let him stay in the garden. When mating season arrived, Gigi became a member of Nonny's small "warm-up act."

The amazing thing is that even in the middle of courting and mating, Gigi never left his mother for very long. Every once in a while he would leave the "warm-up act" and visit his mother, who was now walking around the garden more and eating food with the other cats. When Gigi arrived Three would lick him and somehow let him know she was all right. Only afterward did Gigi return to his male cat activities. Such devotion is probably rare. Whoever knows animals, or just cats, knows that during mating season males only think about one thing. They barely eat and hardly sleep. And here was an adult male cat overcoming his strongest natural instinct to go and see how his mother was doing. When mating season was over Gigi returned to his life in the garden beside his mother.

Almost two years passed and Three's condition remained stable and Gigi remained a loyal son and companion. And then Three gradually grew weaker. She once again spent most of her day in the wicker armchair that remained hers. Gigi sat under the armchair looking dejected and worried, and with good reason.

Three was eating less and less until one night she died in her sleep. I found her in the armchair with Gigi lying near it. When I came closer, Gigi let me pet him, though he usually didn't like it when I touched him. Together we mourned Three's death; her life, though restricted for the most part, was a happy one. This is another example of a cat that enjoyed her life despite its limitations because she lived in the present and didn't cling longingly to the past.

Gigi remained alone in the yard with Nonny as his only friend. But soon enough Nonny's long walks began, which eventually led to Stripy taking his place as leader.

The first time that Stripy walked the garden as the leader of the community, Gigi jumped out through the fence, crossed the road, and took up residence in my neighbor's garden. Two of his uncles lived in that garden, Panther and Tiger.

Now I'd like to finish recounting the tale of the tricolor cats. I'll return to Gigi's story later.

When Three passed away, there was one tricolor female kitten in the garden. She was the daughter of Colomina and the granddaughter of Beauty. Her name was Pretty. Pretty was the only survivor of what was then Colomina's current litter. Like other kittens she climbed into the yard through the opening I had left in the fence, which enabled kittens to jump on the low stone fence and enter the yard. She was an amazingly beautiful kitten, a tabby but with long, thick hair. Like Tete, she also chose to ignore the custom Beauty's family had of not living in the yard. Instead, she made the yard her home. She fit right in with the community and it seemed that everyone admired her beauty. Her face was also different and interesting. It partially resembled a Persian cat, and sometimes it looked like the face of a fox. Given her good looks, it's no wonder she was named Pretty.

Pretty

Pretty managed to escape the first attempt to spay her, got pregnant, and gave birth in the yard to what was probably a full litter. But when she emerged from the secluded corner in which she had given birth, she brought with her only two kittens: a tricolor female kitten, whose colors were more faded but who had longer fur, and an extremely light ginger male with a patch on his chest that was almost white but with a ginger hue. I called the female Light and the male Ginger.

As a cat that grew up without brothers and sisters, Pretty was more a friend and a sister to her kittens than a mother. Apart from the duty of nursing and grooming, which she immediately stopped doing when the kittens reached two months old, she was their friend in every way. The three played together, slept together, and ate together. In short, they had fun together. Pretty seemed to be trying to compensate for her lonely kittenhood.

Light

During the following spring spaying and neutering campaign, Pretty and her daughter Light were caught. This means that Pretty gave birth once, while Light never become a mother. They are both good friends to this day. Their friendship is not as close as the friendship that exists between male kittens or mature males (think of Fluffy and Shushka, for example), but it is certainly rare between mature kittenless females. As we've seen, friendship between female cats usually emerges and revolves around caring for kittens. My two tricolors often sleep next to each other, and many times I see them strolling around together.

Unfortunately, Ginger decided that he didn't like the territory, even though Leo let him stay there. He began to show growing signs of restlessness and disappeared for longer and longer periods of time. Three months ago, he left the yard for good.

When Ginger left, I wondered what would happen to the tricolor females in my community. Two of them were spayed. However, I doubted that one of the few females that had escaped spaying would give birth to a ginger kitten since there were no ginger males around. As I was pondering this issue, a great ginger cat, perfectly amiable, arrived in the yard during mating season. The result was soon apparent. A black female gave birth after six weeks to five black and white male kittens and one tricolor female that greatly resembled the original tricolor cats. Her colors were strong and her coat was short.

Will this kitten survive the renewed winter that we are currently having in the middle of March? I don't know. And if she survives, will she escape spaying? Will the ginger male reappear for the next mating season? In short, will I ever have tricolor kittens again? I don't know.

From what I've learned so far of tricolor females, I know that they are interesting cats, confirmed individualists, good and decisive mothers, and they know how to enjoy their lives. They are certainly cats with a worthy character.

Let's turn now to the ginger cats. Just as tricolor cats are only females, so the ginger cats are only males. I learned this fact not from books but from experience. Only after I saw that all my tricolors were females and all my ginger cats were males did I ask the veterinarian whether this was a known fact and he said that it was.

The first two ginger cats that appeared in our community were Tiger and Panther, Tricolor's offspring. As kittens they were inseparable. As I've mentioned, they didn't get involved in the life of the community even though they spent quite a few months living among its cats. Unlike other male kittens, Tiger and Panther always kept their distance from me. Only rarely did they let me pet them. They tried to include their sister Three in their games, but she, as I've mentioned, preferred to be with her mother or by herself.

Readers might remember that when Tiger and Panther grew up and became real adult males, they were banished from my garden and moved into my neighbor's garden. A year later, my neighbor had them neutered, and so they welcomed Gigi, who was still a male in his prime. My neighbor told me that the moment Gigi arrived in her garden he formed an extraordinary bond with Tiger. At that time, Panther was very friendly with another cat in her garden. I heard that two months after Gigi moved to his new home, he was also neutered and so he and Tiger were finally equals.

When Stripy's reign ended, Gigi and Tiger started coming to the yard. Tiger hadn't visited the place for a long time and it was interesting to see how he examined everything and how he walked around the yard for hours. It took Tiger quite a few visits to feel comfortable in the yard again, and he finally started eating the meals that I provided.

Gigi, on the other hand, happily returned to the place where he had spent most of his kittenhood and youth. He accompanied Tiger everywhere, never leaving him alone. It was as if he sensed that Tiger was feeling out of place and was full of trepidation. But once Tiger adjusted, Gigi walked around the yard as though it was his own. Leo welcomed both of them with open arms.

Gigi

After a few months, Tiger and Gigi relocated to my yard. They found a bed and shared it, and little by little, they began forming relationships with other cats in my community. It doesn't mean that they spent all day in the yard—not at all. Every day they went on walks around the neighborhood, including in my neighbor's garden, and returned to eat and sleep. Gigi was similar to Legs and Grayush in that every day he left the yard sometime in the afternoon, crossed the street, and jumped on the corner of the stone fence of the house across from ours. So every afternoon, when I drove home, I saw Gigi sitting on the fence with Grayush often sitting next to him. Gigi was so consistent with this routine that I would slow down as I drove toward the house to make sure that Gigi was indeed sitting on the fence.

Tiger

In the meantime, I improved my relationship with Tiger, who was a ginger cat through and through. Gigi had white spots, so he wasn't a pure ginger cat. Tiger became much friendlier toward me. He ran to me and accompanied me as I tidied things up in the garden or changed newspapers and blankets in the cat pergola. He came to me to get a hug and a pet and would ceaselessly rub up against me.

What caused this dramatic change? I don't know. Perhaps it was Gigi's influence on him, or the result being neutered. In any case, Tiger and I became fast friends. My friendship with Gigi also grew, and my admiration of him for the way he treated his mother until the day she died only increased my love for him. I also really liked his protective attitude toward Tiger. In this way Gigi became one of my favorite and most respected cats.

This ideal relationship between Gigi, Tiger, and me continued for two years until one unhappy day when I saw while driving home that Gigi was not on the fence. My heart began to beat quickly. I parked the car and ran into the yard to see what was happening. I didn't even bother to bring food with me.

There was no trace of Gigi or Tiger in the yard. For a moment I considered the possibility that Gigi may have been gone because he and Tiger had gone on a long walk together. But reason told me that Gigi wouldn't deviate from his habit of sitting on the fence as he had every day for nearly two years.

I turned to the cat pergola and immediately I saw Tiger lying next to the bed he shared with Gigi. I was afraid to come any closer, but I finally found the courage and stepped forward. I saw Gigi lying in the bed, his posture almost normal, but not quite. I quickly went over to the bed. Only then did I see a trickle of blood dripping from Gigi's mouth. Gigi lay dead in his bed. I think he must have been hit by a car when he crossed the road, and this caused internal bleeding. With his last ounce of strength, he managed to reach his bed and with Tiger by his side, he passed away.

The sadness was terrible. All the cats sensed that something awful had happened. The atmosphere was dark and it was made even more so by Tiger's behavior. After I changed the blanket in the bed he had shared with Gigi, he lay down in it and hardly left. Tiger was in mourning for two weeks. Only when the two weeks ended did he start coming for meals from time to time. He was very thin and I was afraid that he would get sick. I prepared special food that I hoped he would like. But nothing helped. Finally, three weeks after Gigi passed away, I came out into the yard and saw Tiger standing in the garden with Panther by his side. I don't know how Panther found out that his brother Tiger was in trouble. For years, Panther avoided the yard but now he was here, keeping his brother company. Panther's visit lasted for a day and then two, until finally, right in front of me, Panther jumped up onto the fence, followed by Tiger, and the two disappeared into my neighbor's garden.

The next day I went to visit my neighbor and recounted the entire story. She confirmed that to her astonishment, Tiger had appeared in her garden the previous day. She said that he was getting along splendidly with Panther's close friend. I looked out the window and saw all three cats playing in the grass. I was relieved that Tiger had found himself a home and friends once more. But the pain I felt for Gigi—as I have felt for other cats that have passed away—never went away.

Sometimes I feel that the pain is unbearable. I have to remind myself that my street cats' lives were made better by the help I provided and that others like me provide, and that there are street cats that are in a far worse situations. Although the misery of others is no true comfort, in times of distress, when another tragedy strikes my community, I do find some peace in knowing that my cats led beautiful lives.

The last ginger cat that I want to talk about was Red's offspring, whose story I told in the chapter about the pergola infiltrators. This ginger cat was part of a sickly and problematic litter. It was Red's second litter, which she gave birth to when she was still quite small, and the kittens were almost premature. She gave birth to them in a dark corner of the yard, behind a large brick. After a week, I heard the cries of kittens and saw three little, froglike creatures with fur: two kittens were ginger and one was gray.

A difficult period followed during which I assisted Red with raising her nearly premature litter. I gave them baby formula and sugar water and she nursed them as best as she could. She groomed them and lay beside them for days on end. It seemed that we had a chance of saving these small creatures because they began putting on weight and started looking like proper kittens. Then, when they were about five weeks old, they all contracted acute eye infections. The veterinarian supplied eye drops and an ointment and recommended special antibiotics in very small dosages. Everything was done as he instructed, but without much success. The two ginger cats went blind and only the gray kitten managed to retain his eyesight.

I talked to the veterinarian and we decided to try to find adoptive families for the two blind ginger kittens. I brought them to him and to their credit, it must be said that they fought like lions to survive. But when the vet saw the two kittens he told me that one was in critical condition and would probably die soon. And so he did.

The good news was that an adoptive family was found for the remaining blind ginger kitten. I receive reports about him from time to time and hear that he came in for his shots, that he's growing and developing well, and that thanks to the love of his adoptive family he is living a good life. It's nice to know that there are people whose love of animals gives them the strength to adopt a sick blind kitten, and that even in these cases love is the mightiest force.

These days it is Panther, not Tiger, that visits my garden from time to time. Over the years, he has become a chubby, kind cat. And as previously mentioned, a good-natured ginger male has also joined the community. Thanks to his personality, so far he has managed to fit in nicely with the community. He is now one of the males in my leaderless community of cats, and as I've mentioned, if he sticks around, the females that managed to avoid being spayed might give birth to other tricolor and ginger kittens.

Panther

Many people are interested in adopting a ginger cat. Ginger cats seem different to them and much nobler than tabby cats, for example. All that I can say is that, in my experience, ginger cats are just as intelligent as other cats and they are not more affectionate or friendlier than their more common siblings. Ginger cats are also more sensitive and prone to disease. And yet they have certain virtues, just as other cats have their own particular qualities. Perhaps it is best to avoid generalizations, as every cat belongs to a certain group of cats because of its coat color. But every cat has its own distinct personality. In my eyes, this is the important factor, not coat color.

Black and White Cats

Black and white cats include all cats with mostly black fur, but with a small area covered in white fur. The combination of black with white creates strange and unusual patterns sometimes, some black and white cats look like they are wearing Halloween masks. The black color stops sometimes above the eyes, making it look like a cat has thick eyebrows. Other times, the black color appears all the way up to the eyes, but also on the chin, making it look like a cat has a beard. In my eyes, they are all amazingly beautiful and the "costumes" that nature gave them make me happy.

During the first year I observed my community, there was not a single black and white cat present. The community consisted solely of gray cats, gray and white cats, and tabbies. During the second year, a big and beautiful black and white cat managed to join the community. Geezer welcomed him for some reason and made him a member of his "warm-up act" in which the black and white cat played a key role. Several black and white kittens appeared in the next round of litters. All except one were male.

As readers already know, young males are the friendliest cats toward humans. But the friendliest of these are the black and white cats. I've never come across a young black and white male that didn't like being stroked. Many of them jumped onto my knees when I sat in the garden on one of the low stools or in the cats' wicker armchairs. Some of the black and white cats had long fur, and these were the most unbelievably friendly ones, so much so that their personalities seem almost human. One could even talk to them. They emitted sounds that sounded like speech and I often imagined that I could understand them.

Their behavior was a bit riskier than usual. One black and white cat managed to climb up onto the roof of the pergola and from there he must have jumped to our second floor balcony. There was a cupboard there and it turned out that we had left one door open. He settled in the balcony cupboard and fell asleep. He only started meowing when he woke up, tried to climb down, and couldn't find a way to jump back onto the roof of the pergola from the balcony. The cries brought me up there. I opened one of the doors onto the balcony and after much persuasion he found the courage to jump onto the roof of the pergola and from there climbed down the tree to reach the cat pergola. When he finally got down, he ran as if he were possessed straight out of the yard.

I remember one black and white male that always slept inside a bucket in the yard. Once, when I hung the bucket up on a high hook, I was astonished to see later on that he had found a way to climb inside the bucket. The fact that the bucket was hanging in the air didn't stop him from wanting to sleep in his preferred spot.

When the rains came, I was afraid that he would sleep inside the bucket even if it filled with water. True, this doesn't say much about the cat's intelligence, but it just so happened that this black and white cat did jump into the bucket when it was full of rainwater. If I hadn't come and rescued him, he probably would have come down with acute pneumonia.

The black and white kittens from the first two litters befriended each other. They slept together in one bed in what appeared to be a black bundle with a few white patches; it was impossible to tell what was a head, body, or tail.

Kittens rarely left the garden before they reached sexual maturity, but afterward that point they immediately started taking long walks around the neighborhood, which usually ended with their permanent disappearance. The garden could be full of black and white patches of color one week and the next there would be hardly any black and white patterns to be seen.

Blacky

I want to tell the tale of one black and white cat that I creatively named Blacky. Blacky appeared in the garden when he was a kitten in the middle of Nonny's reign. He grew up into a magnificent cat, without having suffered any of the usual kittenhood diseases. During his time, the spaying and neutering program hadn't started yet, so when he was eight months old he became a mature male in every sense. For some reason, Nonny didn't banish him from the territory, but he also didn't make him a member of his "warm-up act". Blacky must have joined the "warm-up act" of another male because he would disappear for days and return exhausted.

Once, after he returned exhausted after a rather long absence, I noticed that he had sores on his legs. I determined that a veterinarian needed to see him. The vet examined him and told me the worst news possible: Blacky had feline AIDS and he must have been born with the disease. The veterinarian told me that although it was possible at that stage to treat Blacky with various drugs and heal his sores, his life would be very short.

I became very depressed. This was such a magnificent cat, loving and loved, yet he was doomed at birth. It seemed utterly unfair to me. My cat-loving friends tried to comfort me, saying that they too had young cats in their gardens with feline AIDS, and these cats lived for at least a few years. None of this made me feel better.

Blacky's long treatment began. He cooperated admiringly, as if he understood that his life depended on the treatment that he was receiving. After a month of constant care, his sores did improve and Blacky got his strength back and resumed his walks. During the following mating season, Stripy was the leader of the community, and he violently banished Blacky from the garden. When two weeks went by and then three and four, I realized that Blacky might come to visit sometimes if he managed to survive, but the yard was no longer his home.

The next part of the story takes place during the second year of Stripy the tyrant's reign. It wasn't mating season in my community and Stripy went to explore other territories. One somewhat rainy winter day, I went out to feed the cats. When the meal was finished, I suddenly heard meows that reminded me of the sounds that Blacky used to make. I looked all over the yard and in the cat pergola, but I couldn't find anything. The sounds continued. It suddenly occurred to me to look up, and that's when I saw Blacky's face; he was standing on the edge of the roof of the pergola. The moment I saw him I called out to him, "Blacky, Blacky," and he sped down the pergola beams and ran to me. I stroked his head and we stood like that for several minutes. The rain stopped and I forgot for a moment that Blacky was sick. I naturally hurried to prepare a plate of food especially for him. After he ate, I instinctively looked at his legs and

saw that again, they were covered with sores, and this time the sores were much larger. I called the veterinarian who told me that this wasn't unexpected and that the disease was progressing. He told me what I could do to make things easier for Blacky.

Because of his thick fur I didn't notice at first how thin Blacky was, nor did I see how weak he became in the face of his happiness and mine. After my conversation with the veterinarian, I went out to the yard again, and this time I saw that Blacky was not doing well at all. I led him to the cat pergola and arranged a bed for him in the corner, where it was warmest. I lined his bed with because I understood that I would have to change them every day. I placed a bowl of water near the bed and after Blacky fell asleep, I returned inside.

I sat and thought about what could be done for Blacky. Unfortunately, the more I thought, the more I realized that his fate was sealed and that all that I could do was try and restore his strength, and give him the necessary medication so he might go out for one more walk, which just might be his last.

I prayed that Stripy wouldn't return soon because it was clear to me that Blacky required a lengthy treatment. It turned out that Stripy had gone on a long journey that time, though this wasn't common for him at the time. He returned ten days after Blacky's arrival, but to my delight, when he saw Blacky in bed or walking hesitatingly around the yard, he didn't attack him and let him stay in the community. Stripy must have felt that this weak and sick cat posed no threat to him. And so Blacky remained in the yard until his condition improved and he began taking short walks. Stripy didn't bother him. It seemed to me that he was sympathetic toward Blacky, which was a trait that I had never attributed to Stripy before.

During the months that Blacky was with us, I spent a lot of time in his company, not only to care for him, but also to relieve his loneliness. Three months after he arrived, exhausted and sick, I went out to the garden and saw that Blacky was gone. I concluded that he had gone for a walk, perhaps a long walk. I was happy that he had the strength for it and was sad that we hadn't said goodbye. Suddenly I heard those familiar sounds. I immediately looked up and there he was, standing on the roof of the pergola looking fuller and healthier. I looked at him and waved. I felt that I was waving goodbye to him. After a few minutes, he quickly descended the wooden beams in his usual way, rubbed up against me for a few minutes, and then turned to the fence and jumped out. That was the last time I saw Blacky—a cat that despite having been born with a chronic condition, bravely fought his disease and lived a full life. For me Blacky is a symbol of all the black and white cats that I've known. They were all very brave, though as I've said, not all of them were very smart. Why do I love these cats more than any other cat? I have no clear answer to this question. I just do.

Foxy

I can't conclude my story of black and white cats without mentioning Leo's sister, a beautiful black and white female named Foxy due to her magnificent tail. Together with Leo, she was born in the garden of the woman who lives across the street from me, and she was spayed by my neighbor. Foxy came to me because for some reason the cats in my neighbor's garden picked on her. For years, she came to all meals and afterward quickly disappeared to some unknown location. Over time, she became affectionate toward me. In fact, it's more than that; she has become trusting.

After one failed attempt at petting her, I no longer try to do so. I am just glad to see her and know that she is well. Though she became part of my garden and later the yard, she has never befriended another cat and I think that she has lived a completely solitary life since the death of her brother Leo. And yet, she doesn't seem miserable to me. But I can't really tell what's in her heart because we are not that close. I haven't succeeded in developing a dialogue with her. It's enough for me that she shows up. This too is love.

Chapter 15: Unusual Cats with Ordinary Names

Green Cat

One spring afternoon the doorbell rang. I opened the front door and there was my neighbor from down the street. This was the neighbor who called the municipal cat catcher when Sophie gave birth in his garden. After that incident, I asked him to let me know if he discovered kittens in his garden again, which is what he was doing that spring afternoon. He told me that a week before he had found two kittens on his second floor balcony, which was off his bedroom. He said they were noisy and messy, and he asked me to help catch them, take them downstairs, and move them to another garden.

He told me he had seen the kittens' mother several times and that she was bigger than any cat that he had ever seen or heard of. It was no wonder that such a large cat could climb up the tree near his house all the way to the second floor and give birth to her kittens there.

I grabbed a cage and followed him to his house. The balcony was used for storage, and in that mess a few large, fat kittens were running about, all of them tabbies. I tried to catch them all, but without much success. I managed to grab two kittens and put them in the cage. The other four kittens hid among the clutter and couldn't be caught.

I took the two kittens down to the neighbor's garden and explained to him that I had to leave them there so their mother could find them. I told him that based on my experience with cats, the kittens were old enough to eat by themselves, and I had no doubt that their mother would move them from the balcony very soon. Since the neighbor was about to go abroad for two weeks, we agreed that if the mother did not remove her kittens from his balcony by the time he returned, I would call a cat catcher.

Two weeks went by. The neighbor returned and I went over to find out where things stood. He happily told me that all the kittens had disappeared. I asked him if he had seen the giant cat again, and he said that he hadn't.

Since I hadn't seen a giant cat in my garden or when I walked around the neighborhood, I thought that my neighbor must have simply seen any typical big cat like Geezer, for example. I forgot all about the huge cat. Then, one morning as I went out to feed the cats, I caught a glimpse of some kind of animal sitting in the corner of the garden. I couldn't quite make it out. I finished distributing the food among the cats and turned to get a proper look at this strange creature. It didn't run away as I stood between it and the food. The animal was indeed a cat, but I had never seen a cat like her or come across a description of such a cat in any book I'd ever read.

The cat, which I assumed was the female my neighbor had described, was a tabby, but of a very unusual kind. Her whole body was marked by large arches, and there was a greenish hue to her coat. She really was huge, almost like a medium-sized dog.

I had no doubt that she had come to eat and was standing there because she was afraid of me. I moved to the side and she approached the food. The cats in my community greeted her with fear and assumed attack postures. She emitted what sounded like a warning growl, went over to one of the plates, and quickly ate, all the while looking back at me every so often.

The moment she finished eating, she leaped—yes, literally leaped— onto the fence, and from there she disappeared outside.

Green Cat did not return more meals that day, but the following morning she again appeared in the corner of the garden we went through the same process. She waited for me to move, then she approached the food, growled a bit, ate, and leaped outside. This continued for several weeks. Every once in a while she missed a day.

Green Cat

I hoped that she would get used to me and begin to trust me so I could get close to her, but this never happened. She remained suspicious of me from day one. After six or seven weeks, it seemed to me that she was getting bigger. I looked at her closely and saw that she was pregnant. Because of her size, her pregnancy didn't show at first, but it was still clear that her shape was different. If truth be told, part of me really wanted her to give birth in my garden or in the cat pergola so I could get close to her and her kittens. But another part of me was afraid of this possibility because there was no guarantee that she would become friendlier toward me. If she gave birth in my garden, she might also become more aggressive toward the cats in the community due to a mother's protective instincts.

Thoughts are one thing, and reality is quite another. After a few weeks Green Cat disappeared for several days and returned thinner than before. It was obvious that she had given birth, but I didn't know where. I hoped it wasn't on my neighbor's balcony again, as I didn't want to be called to deal with the problem.

Green Cat must have learned from her experience with the neighbor. Either she did not give birth in someone's garden, or she gave birth in a garden of a person who cared for her and the kittens. She continued coming once a day for breakfast, ate even more quickly than before, and afterward leaped out of the garden, probably to head back to her kittens.

During all this time, the only progress in our relationship was the fact that Green Cat no longer stood at the edge of the yard, as far away from me as possible, but dared to stand closer to me while she ate. I therefore managed to see her wondrous coat from up close—and it was truly a miracle of nature. The color was indeed brownish green and the arches that covered her whole body created an amazingly beautiful abstract painting. She also began to respond when I called her by her name, Green Cat, and turned her face toward me. The cats in my community slowly got used to her, and she to them. They simply made way for her near the plates and she stopped growling.

And then, just when things began to improve, she vanished. It happened during a particularly rainy week when I was feeding the cats inside the closed cat pergola. She appeared once but didn't dare enter the closed pergola. She seemed quite scared of closed spaces. The next day, when she saw that I was again feeding the cats in the cat pergola, she concluded that this was how things were going to be and she stopped coming. After a couple of months, she reappeared a few times. Then she disappeared again, and she has not returned since.

Naturally, I asked myself where Green Cat might have come from. Since there are no cats like her in Israel—and I verified this with several cat experts—she must have been brought here from another country.

Did she run away from home because she didn't like her owners or her living situation? Or was she abandoned because her owners found it hard to take care of her? Obviously, I have no answers. One thing is clear: as far as I'm concerned, if Green Cat was abandoned by her owners, no matter the reason, this constitutes a crime. One of the cat welfare societies would have been able to provide a much better solution for Green Cat.

I kept wondering what had happened to her. It seemed to me that she was probably doomed to a life of loneliness in our country since our native cats see her as threatening and scary. The only real question is whether she managed to live a decent life despite her forced isolation. In my heart, I hope that she simply lost her way back home, and by some miracle her owners finally found her. Once again, heartache returned—this is the lot of every person who cares for street cats.

White Cat

One day, a six-month-old kitten appeared in the garden out of nowhere. Its coat was completely white. I went out to the yard in the morning as usual and saw a white cat in one of the beds. I approached him carefully, trying not to scare him off, and saw that he was sleeping.

I stood next to him and tried to wake him up by calling to him. I spoke nonsense words quite loudly, but he didn't wake up. I started banging a spoon against a cat food bowl, but the cat continued sleeping. I began to fear that he was dead and only appeared to be sleeping. I bent over and saw that he was breathing normally. I touched him lightly and a miracle happened: he woke up, looked at me suspiciously, and jumped out of the bed. I followed him and placed a plate of food in front of him. He ate ravenously; it looked like he hadn't eaten a decent meal in a long time.

White Cat

After he ate, he strolled around the yard for a bit, looking at the other cats while they looked at him. There was no hostility in the air, but neither was there acceptance. White Cat walked around the yard for about ten minutes until he caught sight of a broom with bristles made from straw. He immediately sat on the broom and went back to sleep.

I admit that I saw nothing unusual in my first encounter with White Cat. It didn't surprise me that he had woken up only to my touch. I thought he must have been sleeping too deeply to be woken up by mere sound.

The next day, when I went out into the yard early in the morning, White Cat was still on his broom. As I distributed the food, he waited until all the cats found themselves a place to eat. Only then did he try to approach the food. After a few tries, he succeeded.

When I went out to the yard in the afternoon, I saw him playing alone with a little stick, looking happy and content. The other cats didn't bother him, but they also didn't approach him. It seemed strange to me that the garden kittens that were his age didn't join his game, but again, I didn't think it was significant. I believed that with time the new stranger would be accepted into the community.

And yet there was something in his behavior that seemed strange to me, though I couldn't put my finger on it. The following day I found him sleeping on the broom again and tried to wake him up by calling his very usual name, White Cat, once more. Only when he didn't wake up did I start suspecting that he might be deaf. I tested my theory by calling out to him several times and by making a racket with all the means available to me in the yard, but he didn't wake up. I touched him again very softly, and immediately he was up and awake.

I called the veterinarian and asked him how I could know for sure whether the cat was deaf. The vet immediately asked me what color the cat was and when I said he was white, he told me that cats that are born perfectly white, without the slightest patch of color, are often deaf. And so it seemed that a deaf cat had arrived in the yard. I padded his broom with a comfortable blanket and I would often hand him a plate of food to save him the trouble of trying to find a place with the other cats.

Days went by and the community got used to White Cat. Sometimes I would even see two tabby kittens playing with him. For White Cat's sake, I hoped that he wouldn't leave the yard, for how could a deaf cat survive out in the world? How would he hear the sound of cars approaching, the bark of a dog from which he must flee, or the cries of children chasing him? Luckily for him and for me he stayed in the yard for several months.

When White Cat arrived I still hadn't started neutering and spaying the cats, but I did want to neuter him. I tried in vain to lure him into a cage. When I realized that I couldn't get him neutered, I saw what was to come. And indeed, when White Cat reached sexual maturity—this was during Stripy's reign—the inevitable happened and Stripy violently drove him out of the yard.

White Cat disappeared and never returned. I have no idea what happened to him. Again, like all those who care for street cats, I fear the worst—namely, that White Cat died because of his deafness. But I also hope for the best. Perhaps he found another garden and has been living there ever since.

Chapter 16: Being a Leader

Through the years, ever since Kitsushi first settled in my garden, the community has had five leaders: Geezer, Nonny, Stripy, Grayush, and Leo.

Much has already been said about Geezer. Here I simply want to add that it was during his reign that the community grew. Under his leadership norms of conduct were formed that would remain during the period preceding the construction of the pergola, and to a large extent even after its construction.

When I think of how Geezer, starting with just one small family, succeeded in actually creating a large community where fellowship and friendship prevailed between different cats, I have to attribute this to the way he led by example. I have no doubt that he served as a role model for all the cats in the community by his relationship with Kitsushi and her kittens, the fact that he almost never engaged in violent confrontations, and by his calm demeanor and self-confidence.

Geezer was the largest cat that I have ever seen, with the exception of Green Cat. His size and well-developed muscles scared away almost every mature male cat that came by during mating season to see if he could get any action. I remember only two incidents when Geezer fought, matching his strength against a rival male and, of course, winning.

From Geezer I first learned about the existence of a leader's "warm-up act." Geezer cultivated a respectable "warm- up act," which meant that some of the males born in my garden could stay even when they reached sexual maturity. The females were very respectful toward Geezer and saw it as a privilege to be courted by him once he concluded his courtship of Kitsushi. Everyone knew that Kitsushi was his "wife" and treated her accordingly.

There is no doubt that Geezer's presence brought a sense of security for all the garden residents: mothers, kittens, and sexually mature males. During Geezer's reign, I still hadn't started neutering and spaying cats. I believed that things would take care of themselves and that the community would not exceed ten to fifteen cats.

Over the years, I learned from experience that cats that are cared for the way my cats were have a greater life expectancy and that unless they are neutered or spayed, their number can increase to such an extent that they become a sanitation issue. For this reason, I became a caretaker who neutered and spayed their street cats once a year, as the idea of neutering and spaying had finally become widely accepted at the time, and the means to carry out such a program became available.

During Geezer's reign, there were seven to ten cats that lived in the garden and fifteen cats that ate there. As I've already mentioned, outsiders didn't dare come into the garden, not even for meals, since Geezer's presence was an absolute deterrence. I could still handle this number of cats, though a new plague descended on the community: fleas. Nevertheless, I managed to control even this problem with flea collars for all the cats that agreed to wear them, and by using flea powder on cats that refused to wear a collar.

I have no doubt that Geezer's reign was the most important period in the community's life and that his contribution to it has been the most significant. Even the fact that he chose to pass on his mantle to Nonny was a good decision, though as we've seen, Nonny was in many respects a different leader from Geezer.

As I've already mentioned, Nonny was an average-sized cat and his presence did not deter outsiders from intruding, nor did he automatically intimidate male kittens that were born in the garden and reached sexual maturity. This is why Nonny learned the art of war—not because he liked violence—and he employed this art against every male that he considered a threat.

Aside from this fact, we've already seen that, like Geezer, Nonny was also very gentle with kittens, nursing mothers, and weak cats. In the first year of his reign, the pergolas hadn't been built yet, but the second year unfolded in a new environment. After the human pergola was built and the cat pergola next to it, the yard cats were left with less open space. Only a few females chose to give birth in the cat pergola. The beds were all in the cat pergola, and the yard, which became much smaller, was intended for games and meals (though meals often took place in the cat pergola during winter).

With this geographic change, the communal bonds were weakened, for many of the cats not only chose to live in other gardens, but also to sunbathe there. In winter, only a few cats liked sheltering from the cold and rain in the houses in the cat pergola. This meant that Nonny exercised his leadership over a community that came together mostly only during mealtimes. And as we saw, Nonny himself liked to leave the yard every so often for anywhere between a week and ten days. All these facts came together and made it easier for a cat that knew Nonny and his habits to depose him.

It happened that toward the end of the second year of Nonny's reign, there arose a rival cat, gray from nose to tail, that had been born in the yard before the pergolas were built. As I've mentioned, his name was Stripy. Nonny was kind and gentle toward Stripy when the latter was a kitten.

Meno

Stripy was abandoned by his mother Meno who, for reasons known only to her, disappeared from the garden with her three kittens and left Stripy behind. It's possible that she forgot him or that she left him deliberately because he was a small and weak kitten.

When Stripy grew up, Nonny didn't see him as a threat for some reason and made him part of his small "warm-up act." It turned out that Nonny had underestimated Stripy. Stripy's difficult upbringing turned him into a particularly ambitious, stubborn, mean, and power-hungry cat. Stripy didn't care about Nonny's kindness toward him as a kitten, and when he felt ready, he challenged Nonny's leadership. The fight between the two took place after Nonny returned from one of his lengthy adventures, finished resting indoors, left the house, and entered the yard. I suddenly heard the sounds of cats fighting. It never occurred to me that it could be Nonny and Stripy. I thought that an outsider had entered the yard and that Nonny was fighting him. The cries grew even

Being a Leader

louder and out of concern for Nonny, I went out into the yard only to find Nonny and Stripy facing each other in combat positions. Their cries lasted for twenty minutes after which the fight must have ended in a draw or in a marginal victory for Nonny. Stripy retired and Nonny was left standing. A group of kittens quickly gathered around him.

But Stripy didn't give up. The fights continued for several weeks. During the final week, the two no longer restricted themselves to a battle of cries and counter-cries, and they moved on to physical violence. I only saw one fight that ended in a draw. But it was clear that Nonny was less determined than Stripy. In fact, it seemed that Nonny's heart wasn't in the fight. It's possible that he figured that Stripy would eventually win, given that Stripy was much younger than he was—though not much bigger in size—not to mention extremely determined.

I think that Nonny gave up. He lost the will to lead. Perhaps he wanted to spend more time exploring the neighborhood, and perhaps he just grew tired of leadership. In any case, when I came out the next morning after the fight that I had witnessed, I saw Stripy standing in the middle of the yard and there was no trace of Nonny. I guessed that the battle was over and Stripy was the winner. An hour later Nonny came home and stayed inside for several days. As I've mentioned, when Nonny finally went back outside, a number of females that did not want to accept Stripy's leadership were waiting for him.

I admit that I did not like Stripy. When he was a kitten, I tried to pamper him and compensate for his sudden abandonment. But he rejected all my attempts to get close to him. He would eat the special food that I had prepared for him, swallow the medicine I administered, but never let me pet him. This is quite unusual for a male and it says quite a lot about Stripy's antisocial personality, which was evident even when he was small. After his mother abandoned him, he never befriended the other kittens or joined in other cats' games. He found himself a corner where he slept, appeared for meals, and ate well. He would leave the yard for short walks and then return to his semi-autistic lifestyle. As I've said, Nonny protected Stripy as a kitten, but Stripy never even showed Nonny any affection. A cat psychologist might have said that having been abandoned suddenly as a kitten, Stripy lived his life in a post-traumatic state. Clearly he wasn't like the other cats. And I personally have no doubt that it was his experiences as a kitten that turned him into such an unusual cat.

Stripy's reign was fraught with violence. He introduced strict rules and an iron discipline to the community. Remember that his reign occurred after the pergola was built. He lorded over the cat pergola and the permanent residents in the yard. Unlike Geezer and Nonny, Stripy disliked the weak and admired the strong.

In contrast to his predecessors, he established the custom that he must be the first to approach food and select a plate. No other cat could move toward the food before he started eating. More than once, when a particularly young kitten that didn't understand the meaning of this hierarchy ran over to the food before Stripy chose a plate, Stripy would run him off in disgrace. It didn't matter which cat dared approach the food before Stripy took his place. He drove all of them away. Sometimes he did it through physical violence, such as by slapping a cat with his front paw.

The two years Stripy reigned over the community were the most miserable. The residents of the yard and the cat pergola abandoned their homes. Every male that reached sexual maturity left the territory and didn't even dare return for meals. Even some of the females chose to live somewhere else and came to me only for meals. Few kittens were born in the yard during Stripy's reign and mothers would arrive with their kittens only once they were at least two months old and required solid food in addition to milk. To me it seemed that even the kittens' games were more subdued, as if their mothers had warned them not to cause any disturbance that could upset Stripy. The only male whose presence Stripy tolerated, and who was the lone member of Stripy's "warm-up act," was Grayush. Perhaps Stripy needed Grayush and his magnificent singing voice beside him as he courted a female, because Stripy himself was markedly untalented in this area.

Stripy would patrol the cat pergola and yard several times a day, just like a general assembling his troops for formation. It seemed that Beauty was the only cat that Stripy respected, and when he saw her and her kittens in the yard eating, lying in the sun, or playing, he didn't interfere. Beauty was also not afraid to approach the plates of food right after I put them down. She didn't wait for Stripy's permission. As was her custom, Beauty never lived or gave birth in the garden. She usually left the yard with her kittens right after eating, so it's hard to say how the two would have gotten along if Beauty had been a permanent resident of the cat pergola and the yard.

Stripy had almost exclusive rights over females during mating season, with the exception of Grayush as his lone "warm-up act." All other males born in the garden ran away the moment they reached sexual maturity, and Stripy would immediately drive away any male from outside. As a result, the pergola began to fill up with gray cats. This was the one thing that made me happy during Stripy's reign, for ever since Kitsushi's time, I've had a great fondness for gray cats. My happiness was short-lived, however. The gray kittens were mostly males, with two exceptions, and they ran away at a young age.

Unlike his predecessors, Stripy hardly took time off from the yard to explore the neighborhood for a few days. He seemed afraid of being usurped by another cat if he went away for too long. Usually he went out for a walk in the morning and returned in the evening. I was therefore very surprised when, in the middle of the summer, sometime in early August, Stripy disappeared. A day passed, and then a second. A week passed and then two weeks and still there was no trace of Stripy. Naturally Grayush filled in as leader in his absence, given that he was the only mature male in the yard.

Three weeks later, I went out into the yard one day and saw a gray, thin, shabby cat. At first I didn't recognize Stripy. He had changed so much. When he started walking, however, I recognized his gait and I understood that this was indeed Stripy, or more precisely, what remained of Stripy. Stripy was five years old, so I didn't think that he was ill. Instead, I thought he must have been worn out by his long journey. I felt sorry for him and placed a plate heaped with premium food in front of him. For the first time in his life, Stripy gave me a grateful look, but he ate sparingly. During dinner, he went missing again.

After that day I saw Stripy passing through the yard several times a day and it didn't take long to realize that he was sick and dying. Every time he came by, he looked worse. This is probably the worst part about caring for street cats—seeing them wither away.

Getting him into a cage so I could bring him to the veterinarian was obviously an impossible mission. Even when he was at death's door, he wouldn't let me touch him. The last time I saw Stripy, he was patrolling the yard and the cat pergola at length, sitting down every few minutes and looking around him. He probably sat down because he didn't have any strength left. But when he sat and slowly looked around, it seemed to me that contrary to the way most cats live the moment, he was replaying in his mind the heyday of his reign over the community in the yard. I had no doubt that Stripy was taking leave of his kingdom. After that day, Stripy was never seen again. He must have gone off to die in some secluded corner.

Grayush, who had taken over the role of leader during the last month of Stripy's life, continued leading the community. And amazingly enough, even though Grayush was relatively small and was certainly not an impressive-looking cat—quite the opposite, in fact—cats from outside did not dare take him on. As I've mentioned, his glorious voice must have driven them away.

Slowly, the atmosphere in the yard and in the cat pergola returned to normal. Males that were born in the yard remained there, and a few females returned from other gardens to give birth and live in the yard, or at least to spend more time there. More kittens were born in the yard again and they could be seen romping around. Grayush adopted all of Nonny's habits, except for his violence toward males from outside. He loved playing with kittens and teaching them new tricks. During mealtimes, Grayush waited for everyone in the community to find a place first, and he was always last to take his place to eat. He also helped the weak and the shy. Above all, Grayush sang beautifully all year round, not just during mating season. He would go up onto the roof of the pergola, sit there to observe his territory with compassion and joy, and raised his voice in song.

This was indeed a happy time. Nevertheless, there was one problem that dampened my joy. The number of cats had multiplied, and though I called the cat catcher every spring, only some could be caught to be neutered or spayed. I was afraid of my neighbors' wrath and I still vividly remembered the horrific tragedy of the cat transfer (I still can't forget it to this day).

I therefore decided to try to launch an adoption campaign. With the help of members of the cat rescue society Helping Cats, a few people came to the yard, most of them women, and chose a cat. If the cat chosen was friendly, I immediately placed it inside the cage that the hopeful cat owner was asked to bring along, and the human and the cat went on their way. This is how I managed to place nine cats in happy adoptive homes, most of them kittens on the brink of maturity and not more than six months old.

Using this dual approach—neutering and spaying (luckily that year we managed to catch most of the females) and promoting adoption—I managed to keep the number of cats that ate in my yard to between fifteen and twenty. The number of kittens in the pergola did not exceed seven or eight, and there were only one or two litters at most since most females had been spayed.

Gradually most of residents and visitors in the yard were spayed or neutered. There were at most two sexually mature males around Grayush during mating season, born to females that we couldn't catch. There might not have been much mating during Grayush's reign, but there was certainly much love.

For two years, the community lived peacefully under Grayush's leadership until he decided that he had had enough of being a leader, as I described in a previous chapter. He was already seven years old and he wanted to make time for short walks in the sun and among the flowers, as well as for more sleep and rest. It's possible that his body was beginning to weaken, but he didn't show any outward symptoms.

Grayush was meticulous in his choice of successor. He selected a huge and beautiful tabby who had long hair and was neutered. Yes, neutered. The tabby and his sister, Foxy, whom I've mentioned, came to us from the garden of the neighbor across the street. I've mentioned her on occasion, as she also fed street cats, albeit in a smaller operation than mine.

I don't quite know how the change in leadership came about, but there was a transition period of several months in which Grayush was seen everywhere with Leo, which was the very unoriginal name that I gave that big and handsome tabby. After the transition period, Grayush disappeared for three days for the first time in his life, and Leo unsurprisingly took his place.

Leo was the last leader to reign supreme over the community. It made sense that Grayush chose a neutered male to take over his role, for at that time, most of the cats in the community where either neutered or spayed.

Leo's leadership style was very similar to that of Grayush and Nonny. He was kind and generous toward his subjects, helped the weak, and made sure that I took care of the sick. He had a paternal attitude toward male cats that escaped neutering but that had been born in the pergola. Even though he was not sexually active, during mating season he led the group of young males and taught them the customs of courtship, chasing away any male cat from outside that tried to enter the yard. Most cats from outside were afraid of his size and didn't dare come closer, but some sensed that he was neutered and decided to try their luck. Toward these interlopers Leo used violence, just like Nonny did, and Leo forcefully chasing away a male that threatened his leadership was not a pretty sight.

During Leo's reign, the community became closer and maintained a steady number of about fifteen to twenty cats that regularly came for meals, as well as another seven cats that lived in the yard and cat pergola, or at least spent a significant amount of time there. There were only one or two litters. Since I diligently continued spaying and neutering cats, the picture didn't change. Leo helped by preventing cats from outside—males and females that might have been sexually active—from joining the community.

Leo's reign ended like Stripy's with his death. When he accepted leadership, Leo was already seven years old and had been neutered for two years. Surviving for nine years is an impressive accomplishment for a street cat. Unlike Stripy, who disappeared during the last month of his life and reappeared for his goodbye patrol just before he died, Leo spent his last weeks and days in the community. His dwindling fur revealed his condition and it was clear to me that his days were numbered. Yet even when he looked quite bad, he still walked around the yard and lay in the sun, warming himself for hours. One day he went away, never to return. Like Nonny, Stripy, and many other cats, he chose to die in an isolated spot and not in his home.

After Leo's death, no other cat took his place as leader. A community that is mostly neutered and spayed is probably not very attractive. Sometimes males from outside join the community to eat. Most of them are rejected by the community, but every so often, a new cat is welcomed with open arms. I haven't yet managed to figure out how the selection process is conducted, but one thing was clear: all new cats have an easy-going personality. Needless to say, new males don't stay in the community for very long because there aren't enough females during mating season (no more than two or three every season). After a few days they usually move on to other hunting grounds.

Today the community operates more like a democracy. There is no strict feeding hierarchy, though it sometimes seems to me that special respect is shown toward the very old and very young cats. There is hardly any fighting, but the joy and cheer that characterized the community before the neutering and spaying program are also gone.

As I've mentioned, there is undoubtedly a clear conflict between the interests of humans and the interests of a normal community of cats. By ensuring that cats won't breed and multiply, we create unnatural communities of street cats. It is true that spayed and neutered cats live healthier, longer lives, but their natural way of life is lost.

I sometimes think that a day will come when no street cat will escape neutering or spaying. This will be the end of street cats. They will stop breeding. I'm always told that this day will never come because there are always some street cats that manage to avoid the cat catcher. But who knows? With advances in medical technology, a method of universal neutering and spaying could be developed, and then what? Even today everything is quieter and cleaner, at least on the street where I live, which has been the home of two thriving communities of cats. But the street is also less teeming with life.

Chapter 17: Dying Cats

From all my cat stories up to this point, readers have learned by now that when a cat feels that its days are numbered, it will do one of two things. Either it will stay and die in its home, or it will choose to die elsewhere—if it left its birthplace to move to another territory, it may return to its birthplace to die, or the cat will choose to die in a strange, isolated corner somewhere.

Some of the cats in my community whose day had come chose the first way, and others the second. Some, like Blacky, combined the two by returning to their home before they died to spend some time there and then, when they felt the end coming, they disappeared. Nonny chose to go out on one last grand exploration and die away from home, and so did Pishoosh. Grayush, Beauty, and Colomina, on the other hand, chose to die at home.

Some cats, like Gigi, didn't choose, because death found them suddenly at home or close by. Some of these cats must have wanted to return home, but were run over or fell down from exhaustion on their way back to their final resting place.

We also had some adult cats from outside—all of them male—that came to our garden to spend their final weeks there, and finally die in the garden. There were five of these visitors over the years. I'll tell of one of them now, a black and white cat that was probably quite old when he came to me exhausted and sick.

I want to stop here for a moment and address an interesting question: How do sick and healthy cats alike know how to find a garden with food, a warm bed, medical care, and even a closed cat house to sleep in during winter? Throughout the years, many cats have tried to join my cat community, which accepted a few of them and rejected the rest. Do cats simply enter every garden they come across systematically and check what it has to offer? This is a plausible, reasonable explanation. Alternatively, it's possible that word gets around somehow that there are good living conditions in certain spots, at least among the cats in the neighborhood. The second explanation seems less likely because it assumes that cats can share information with each other. However, I think that the more unlikely option is the right one. I think that cats communicate the presence of a friendly garden to other cats in a variety of ways.

The message can be transmitted through imitation. For example, a cat from outside that sees a neighborhood cat running to a particular garden will run after it to see where the cat is going in such a hurry. The message can be transmitted when a cat passes by our garden and hears the sounds of happy cats. Upon hearing this, he jumps into the garden to see what's happening. And sometimes one friend brings another, which happened with Pishoosh and Shushka. In any case, I believe, or want to believe, that our garden has gained a reputation for being a good place for street cats.

To return to our story, one day an old black and white cat arrived at our door. It was early autumn and there were no empty cat beds. Then, to my astonishment, one of the tabby kittens deliberately got up from his bed and joined his brother in another bed. The old cat immediately entered the empty bed and fell into a deep sleep. Only when I looked at him up close did I see how thin he was and that he had difficulty breathing and suffered occasional coughing fits.

I left him alone to sleep and recuperate a little. I used this time to call the veterinarian and tell him about the sick cat. I also told him that I didn't want to bring the cat in because the cat didn't know me and I was sure that despite his weakness he would run away if I tried to put him in a cage. If I scared him away like this, he would be deprived of the warmth, food, and medical care that I could offer. The vet advised me to do what I already knew was right, but I wanted someone to confirm my decision. The vet suggested that I give the cat wide-spectrum antibiotics that I kept for cases of undefined illnesses in cats. I should make sure that his bed was well padded with blankets and I should feed him special dietary food. If he didn't have feline AIDS or some other terminal disease, he would recover, but if not, at least we would have tried to save him.

I did as I was told. The cat adamantly refused to touch the food with the antibiotics as well as the dietary food. He enjoyed his warm bed and small amounts of regular cat food. As days passed, he spent more and more time sleeping, until one morning I found him dead in his bed.

The black and white cat was with us for almost two months. During this time, he enjoyed complete rest, for none of the cats bothered him, as well as free access to as much food as he could eat, for none of the cats interfered with him reaching the food. He passed the final months of his life in my community of cats, which behaved toward him in an exemplary manner. This was also how the community treated the other four dying cats that came to us. I only hope that if any of the males that were born in my garden and forced to leave ever reached a similar state, they too found a warm and sympathetic place where they could spend the remainder of their days and die in peace.

I have no doubt that taking in dying cats is one of the greatest mitzvahs, or acts of kindness, performed by those who care for street cats. An equal kindness is to put a dying cat to sleep to spare him those final days or hours of suffering.

I cannot conclude this chapter without saying something about animal euthanasia. In my opinion, the decision to put an animal to sleep is the joint responsibility of the owner and the veterinarian. It is up to the owner, who knows the animal better than the veterinarian does, to determine just how much the animal is suffering. And the same applies to people who care for street cats. If a cat is in pain, it is the responsibility of the owner or caregiver to bring the animal to the vet and discuss the possibility of euthanasia together. If the animal is not suffering but is merely dying peacefully, causing hardship only to the owner or caregiver who cannot bear to see a beloved animal withering away, well, in that case, I think that it is our duty to overcome this feeling and let the animal die in peace in its natural surroundings. It is the veterinarian's job to make sure, when an animal is brought to the clinic, that there is indeed nothing that can be done to save it.

Whenever I see a suffering cat, I try to catch it to bring it to the vet. If it lets me catch it, I try to bring it to the vet, who then determines if the cat can recover. Since I have every confidence in my current vet and know that he'll do everything possible to save a cat before suggesting that we put it down, I accept his recommendation without hesitation. However, when a cat's condition doesn't improve despite caring for him according to the veterinarian's instructions, and when I am sure that the cat is dying painlessly without distress, I let it die in its natural environment. These cats usually pass away in their sleep, lying in their beds.

I believe that my behavior is not unusual in this matter, and I have no doubt that many people who care for street cats do the same. As I've repeatedly mentioned, one of the greatest trials for anyone caring for street cats is to see them wither away, or die, or be put to sleep. A person really has to love street cats to be able to continue caring for them for years and years, all the while experiencing with them all the hardships described in this book.

I've said it before, but it's worth repeating: caring for street cats is an extremely worthy moral endeavor. Therefore it's no wonder that it is wondrous and amazing as well as difficult and exhausting.

Chapter 18: So Now What?

This book has told of the formation and life of a single community of street cats as it evolved over fourteen years. My intention was never to offer a set of scientific observations, but rather to describe the life of the community and my involvement with it.

As I was writing this book, I underwent an extremely intense emotional experience. All the emotions of the past decade and a half came back to me, and I experienced them all over again in a period of just a few months. It wasn't easy. In fact, sometimes it was very hard. While outside in the yard and in the cat pergola, the life of the community continued as usual, the spirits of its members that died or vanished over the years filled the house and, most importantly, my soul. I considered quitting a few times, but my goals in writing this book helped me continue.

First, I wish to introduce people to street cats, to let them know who they are, and how interesting and varied they can be.

Second, I have a burning desire to correct people's misconceptions about street cats. People think that because street cats live their lives in a world that appears closed to us and because they seem able to fend for themselves, it's not possible to form an emotional bond with a street cat. This is a mistake. They cannot live a decent life without us. And what they need from us is not only food, but also loving care, which they can repay in kind.

As I was writing the book and reliving the past fourteen years, the plight of street cats became even more apparent to me. Due to the comfortable weather in Israel and the absence of truly harsh winters, quite a large number of street cats live in our gardens. This is not the situation in cold countries, where there are practically no street cats and only domestic house cats. In my country, the number of cats in our streets is substantial. Until quite recently, however, they had absolutely no rights. It is only the kindness of people sensitive to the plight of the weak in general and to the suffering of animals in particular that help these cats a little. Here and there people feed street cats and even give them medicine, and in extreme situations, like a car accident, take them to the veterinarian.

Yet the kindness of the few is but a drop in the ocean. Little by little, society is beginning to understand that we have a moral obligation to care for street cats. Various animal welfare societies have been established to address the needs of street cats and public awareness of this issue has increased, largely because of the work of these societies. There is no doubt that we need to strengthen these organizations, for they play a key role in shaping public opinion about street cats.

It's important to me to clearly state what I see as our ultimate goal: we should strive to make most people aware of their moral obligation to aid street cats and do so willingly and with empathy. Cats form a society that exists alongside our human society and they deserve to have their rights protected. Indifference and denial must stop.

I wish for a future where each of us recognizes the street cats in our neighborhood, knows their hardships, and helps them to the best of our abilities. We might even name them.

Even if my wishes seem fantastical—I'm sure some think they are—I present them unhesitatingly to readers as worthy goals. Where there is a dream and the dream is a moral one, more and more people will rise, willing to fight to make it a reality.

The End

ACKNOWLEDGMENTS

I want to thank all those who helped me take care of my street cats throughout the years: my neighbor, Naomi Zabar, the Friday ladies who came to feed the cats, and the neighbors who lent a hand in emergencies.

I am also grateful to the following people: the veterinarian who stood by me during the middle of the period described in this book, Dr. Roni Kalman; the veterinarian who has been standing by me during the past few months, Dr. Shalom Haimovitz; the members of the cat welfare society Helping Cats (Yad Lehatool) and the Society for the Prevention of Cruelty to Animals (SPCA), who helped me arrange adoptions; the staff at the SPCA clinic, who gave emergency care to cats that were run over; to my family for their acceptance of all that is involved in caring for street cats; and to all those who care for street cats, simply for being there.

Finally, this book would not have been published in English were it not for the unfaltering support of Aviva Cantor, and I want to thank her for believing in this project.